HOPE

20 Real-Life Stories of Journeys out of the Darkness into the Light

We want to hear from you. Please send your comments about this book using the email -

carmen@jesusreignsmission.co.uk

Copyright © 2020 by Carmen Lascu

All rights reserved.

Carmen Lascu asserts the moral right to be identified as the author of this book. No part of this publication may be reproduced or transmitted in any form or by any means, electronic or mechanical, including photocopy, recording or any information storage or retrieval system without the prior permission of the author, except for brief quotations in reviews.

Unless otherwise indicated, biblical quotations are from New International Version.

Several names in this book have been changed to protect their privacy.

This book is dedicated to you.
It is no accident that you are reading this book.
God, the Creator of all things, had planned this
moment because He wants to help you.
There is HOPE

The people that shared their stories in this book found hope in God. He restored their lives after deep depression, suicidal thoughts, physical and sexual abuse, drug addiction, excessive drinking, abusive marriage, grief, New Age, witchcraft, and demonic oppression.

ENDORSEMENTS

"I have known Carmen for several years now. In that time I have seen her continue to grow as a passionate follower of Jesus, a strong believer in the Word of God, and a lady highly committed to ministering the gospel of Jesus to everyone she can – with an emphasis on the Holy Spirit's leading and physical healing. Her example is inspirational, and I welcome her contribution to the body of Christ in the UK in this season".

Paul van Essen,

Senior Leader - Greater Life Church,

Staines, UK

"I never tire of reading stories of lives radically changed by Jesus. This book is packed full of such encounters. As you read these testimonies, my prayer is that you will be freshly inspired to go out and share the Good News of Jesus".

Janet Johnston

Pastoral worker – King's Community Church

Southampton, UK

"Revelation 19:10 says that 'the testimony of Jesus is the Spirit of prophecy'. So when we share what Jesus has done, it's as if we are calling more forth, it's like saying, "Do it again God." The testimonies in this book carry great power. Carmen has a very pure heart before the Lord. He is using her to encourage regular people, just like you, to walk in the power and authority of Jesus, through love, every day everywhere you go".

C. Scott Gilbert

Firestorm United Ministries

Virginia Beach, USA

3

ACKNOWLEDGEMENTS

I thank God for the privilege of writing this book and that He connected me with these amazing people that shared their stories of hope. I also want to thank the amazing women and men who shared their testimonies to help others overcome the problems they face in their lives.

Special thanks to my husband and daughter for their love and support, as they encourage me to do what God asks me to do.

I am also grateful for the pastors and ministers that helped me grow: Andy Johnson – King's Community Church, Southampton; Paul Van Essen – Greater Life Church, Staines; Andy Chapman – Riverside Vineyard Church, Feltham; Liam Parker – Flow Church, Staines.

Special thanks to other ministries I have learned from or attended their events - Global Awakening, Lifestyle Christianity, Vineyard Institute, The Last Reformation, Andrew Wommack, John G Lake, Derek Prince, Kenneth Hagin, Kenneth Copeland Ministries to name a few.

CONTENTS

INTRODUCTION

There is a moment when you start wondering if life is more than what you have been doing until now. Depression, stress, anxiety, are factors that influence not only our health and wellbeing but our life entirely. We cannot function well socially, but also mentally and physically, without love and peace. We all need this.

There are lots of teachings and techniques that promise to help you overcome your problems but, even though they may look right, they do not solve the main issue; the change must start from the inside. As a man thinks in his heart, so is he. The heart must change first. All religions and experts in personal development would agree with this.

Thankfully, there is a way out of the problems and circumstances you may face at the moment. God can turn things around for you. I believe He would do this because He loves you.

The stories shared in this book belong to people I met in different circumstances, so God had it all planned long before He asked me to write this book. They all had real-life problems like drug addiction, sex, excessive drinking, abusive marriages, suicidal thoughts, sicknesses, physical abuse from parents, witchcraft, and demonic attacks. They had terrible issues, and, at that time, they could not see any way out. But, eventually, they found the light, and now their lives are back on track. They have all been taken out of the darkness and brought into the light, living healthy and purposeful lives today. Things changed for them after they cried out to God in desperation and turned to Jesus, hoping that He is alive, and He can help them. There is no greater love than the love of God.

My story is different. I had a normal childhood and did not get into trouble when I grew up, but despite having everything I was not happy. I found my God-given purpose after I turned to God and asked Him what He wants me to do.

There is HOPE. I encourage you to read this book with an open heart. I am still in awe of the miracles God did in these people's lives.

Since Jesus died for all sins, there is nothing that God cannot forgive. *"I am the way and the truth and the life. No one comes to the Father except through me"* said Jesus to his disciples and us today, as recorded in the Bible in John 14:6.

8

There is a way to find love, joy, peace, and see your life restored, but to see a total transformation you will have to be open to the idea that God is real, and that He may love you and He may want to help you. I say 'may' in case you do not believe this at the moment.

I believe you did not open this book by accident. God is using it to reveal His power to transform lives. He can help you, as well. Nothing is impossible for Him. Consider this moment a wake-up call and start seeing things you cannot see with your natural eyes. The problem you have has deeper roots, but God wants to heal them and take them away from you.

This book came into existence because God told me to write it to help people see that there is hope and that Jesus has the power to transform lives. He can change your life as well if you are willing to let Him do it.

You may wonder why God would turn His face toward you and help you. He would do this because He loves you so much that over 2,000 years ago He sent His only Son, Jesus, to pay the price for all the bad things you did in your life (the Bible calls them sins). He was crucified and resurrected so that you can be forgiven and have a personal relationship with Him.

9

Some people say this was cruel, but I want to say that this is love. God did not want us to live (here and for eternity) separated from Him, so He made a way to reconcile us to Him, to have the same relationship He once had with Adam and Eve.

Jesus is the bridge to Father, but He also transforms lives. Every story shared in this book testify how their lives changed after they allowed Jesus to take control of their lives. If you struggle to stop taking drugs, had enough of feeling depressed, or cannot see a way out of the circumstances you are in, I believe Jesus can help you. Give Him a try. You have nothing to lose.

I have seen it many times. Because of Jesus' death and resurrection, we can receive God's forgiveness. All we have to do is to repent for our sins, turn away from them, and turn to God. Even if you find it hard to stop doing the wrong things you may do at the moment, that's ok. Jesus will welcome you with open arms and help you be free.

The change starts when you give your life to Jesus and allow Him to help you. For a radical transformation, I recommend you get baptised and receive the Holy Spirit, who will empower you for more extraordinary things.

You did not come into this world by accident; God chose you. He wanted you to be born. God loves you and has an excellent plan for your life. He sees you wonderfully made and worthy of being loved and be accepted into His family.

God so loved the world (including you) that He gave His one and only Son, that whoever believes in Him shall not perish but have eternal life. - John 3:16

***

As you read this book, I pray that the God of our Lord Jesus Christ, the glorious Father, may give you the Spirit of wisdom and revelation, so that you may know Him better. I pray that the eyes of your heart may be enlightened so that you may know the hope to which He has called you, the riches of His glorious inheritance in his holy people, and His incomparably great power for us who believe. That power is the same as the mighty strength He exerted when He raised Christ from the dead and seated Him at his right hand in the heavenly realms, far above all principality and power and might and dominion, and every name that is named, not only in this age but also in that which is to come.

Prayer from Ephesians 1:17-21

JAMES - Sexual abuse led to drugs, witchcraft, and worshipping Satan

By the age of 13, I was sexually abused by two older guys who followed me into toilets and started sexually abuse me. It left me confused, upset and angry, not just outwardly but also inwardly.

Mum and dad were believers, and they were praying for me daily, but I did not know Jesus, and I took some bad decisions when I was young.

By the time I was 17, I had found myself being very violent towards others. My parents knew something happened, but they did not know what I was up to.

After the sexual abuse, I started to get depressed because deep down within me, I felt empty. Some friends introduced me to solvents and drugs, but this did not help. I felt empty and more depressed.

Looking for power

During that time, I wanted to get involved in witchcraft because of the power behind it. It all started when I saw my friends playing with the Ouija board. I understood the high power when I have seen windows and glass bottles break.

In all this time I was searching for something. I was looking for the real truth that I could anchor my life on and be able to walk in power. I tried to find my identity in the Ouija board, but I found myself spiralling into depression.

I turned to devil worshipping after feeling empty with the Ouija board. I said to Satan "I give you my life, my all, my emotions, my thoughts, my heart and my soul. You can have all of me".

I worshipped Satan regularly. I remember I would go into my bedroom and begin to worship him. I brought books on sadism and studied the life of a Satanist. Despite doing this, I felt even more empty than I did before.

Seeing that worshipping Satan did not help, but it made me feel worse, I became interested in becoming a witch. I thought this could be the answer. I heard many stories about witches, and the practice of being a witch looked attractive to me, so I started searching how to do this.

During this time, I started hearing voices telling me to kill myself. I had suicidal thoughts to the degree where one night I took a long sharp knife and held it against my wrist. I could not do it, but I screamed out "if you are real, God, show yourself to me". Deep down, I felt I came to the end of myself.

I was still searching for the truth, and no matter what I tried, I did not find it.

Heaven and hell became real

After that day, I had three spiritual experiences within a month, which revealed Jesus to me.

The first experience I had, I found myself in a pitch-black room, and then I saw a gate before me that looked like a set of prison gates. I felt dragged through these gates, down a dark tunnel, and thrown into a cell. While this was happening, I heard people screaming for help. I felt such a fear that I shouted 'Jesus'.

Suddenly I was taken up to another gate, but this time it was different. I saw the gate slightly open, and I could see a crystal-clear river and luscious green grass. I felt waves of peace and waves of joy wash through me. Then I woke up feeling confused about what I dreamt.

The second dream happened a few days later. In the dream, I saw myself laid out on the floor, and I could see

14

stairs coming from above. I started to see people walking down and up the stairs when I saw the last person. He stopped and looked at me and said, "your first part of your first dream is part of your eternal destiny".

I belted out of bed, totally shaken by this dream. I did not know what to do.

God arranged for me to hear the Gospel

A few days later, I spoke to a friend of mine who invited me to a gospel meeting.

I went to the gospel meeting, and the preacher explained that God so loved the world that He sent his only Son, for whoever believes in him shall not perish but have life everlasting. This truth deeply rooted in my heart. The preacher went onto saying that Jesus said, *"I am the Way the Truth and the Life"* (John 14:6). When I heard this, my heart connected and I realised that I was not just looking for truth and life, I was looking for Jesus because Jesus is the way, the truth, and the life. For me, it was not enough to know about Jesus but to know Jesus as the WAY, the TRUTH, and the LIFE.

He continued explaining how Jesus took up himself our pain and our suffering, and how He was pierced with nails for our sinful nature. He was crushed under the

15

weight of our sinful nature. He also said that the punishment that Jesus took upon himself brought us peace, and by his wounds, we are healed.

As the guy explained about the sufferings of what Jesus went through, I felt the pain Jesus might have gone through. At this point I fell to my knees and cried out "Jesus, you can have all of me". Instantly, my violence began to subside, and, within a matter of weeks, I become a man of peace.

Instantly, the power of God destroyed

- the addiction of drugs and now I stand before you as a free man;

- the power of the witchcraft and now I walk in real truth;

- the suicidal thoughts, and now my mind is renewed in Him.

Today I am a man who is free from the past. I am now walking in real Truth and Power.

I do not know where this lands in your life but if you read what God has done for me, expect He can do more for you too.

I had to choose to say YES to Jesus and, likewise, you have the option to say YES to Him. The Bible declares – "Today is the day of Salvation". This is your day of Salvation.

So, if you are choosing to say YES to Jesus, say this prayer - "Jesus, I know that I haven't been walking with you. I give you my heart, my life, my all to you, and I receive your love, your power, and eternal life. I choose to walk in your way. I choose to walk in your truth and the life you have for me".

If you said that prayer, I would like to welcome you into the Kingdom of God.

Jesus answered, "I am the way and the truth and the life. No one comes to the Father except through me.

John 14:6

ROZ – Rescued from New Age, depression, and suicidal thoughts

I believe there are two types of depression, and I had experienced both in my life.

One is where the anguish, the hopelessness, the darkness is all-consuming. You can see no way out. The pain of living is so intense, and you believe suicide is the only way out.

The other kind of depression is where there are no emotions involved. You feel dead. You feel absolutely nothing and want nothing from your life. Zombie-like. Empty inside. You experiment with everything to find peace. From a place of despair, you will do anything to feel something.

In the last ten years of my life as an alcoholic, from age 30 to 40, I was suicidal and did attempt suicide.

I experienced the second type of depression after my beloved mother died. Four years after her passing, I was empty inside.

When I cried out to God to help me during both bouts of depression, he rescued me! He reached down to me on both occasions and pulled me out of the quicksand of my despair.

There is no shame in addiction. There is no shame in depression.

It is only when the Holy Spirit lives in you that you understand that you are in spiritual warfare. The veil of deception is removed from your eyes. God is real. Satan is real. You are either in the dark with Satan or in the light with Jesus. It is one or the other.

Occultism, alcohol, and suicidal thoughts

Here is my story.

I was brought up Catholic, so always believed in God, but not once was I told that to become part of God's family, to be saved, you must repent, have full immersion baptism, and receive the Holy Spirit.

By my twenties, I owned and used tarot cards and had occult books, would read about astral travelling, aliens and the supernatural. I was a binge drinker as soon as I started drinking alcohol, and once I started, I could not stop. I lost my beloved dad during this time, and

19

alcohol numbed the pain. It would be years later that I would properly grieve the loss of my amazing dad.

By 30, I was an alcoholic. I drank morning, noon and night while working full time and pretending to be normal. For seven years I was taking Propranolol for my anxiety and went through bottles and bottles of Rescue Remedy. My anxiety was constant even on the medication. I was suicidal for about seven years. I even tried to commit suicide but was found by my mother and brought to the hospital.

I got sober at 40 through AA (Alcoholics Anonymous) and consistent hourly/daily prayer. After three months, my anxiety disappeared completely. Thank You, Jesus!!! I had eight wonderful years sharing a flat with my mum. I travelled a lot and felt in control. But when my life seemed to go well, I pulled away from God and became addicted to yoga - Hatha yoga, Bikram yoga, Kundalini yoga. There was always a lost, empty feeling inside me. I qualified as a yoga teacher, but then inexplicably lost all interest in yoga. By this time I was a workaholic, needed sleeping tablets to sleep (for five years), had numerous psychic readings and hypnosis sessions, reading astrology, crystal, the law of attraction and feng shui books, and using Smudge Sticks to 'clean' my aura. I walked around with crystals in my pockets. I was still trying to 'fix' myself.

I lost my beloved mum before 50. Through grief and exhaustion, I locked myself away for two years. I had zero interest in the world. Absolute Zero Interest. I had been to three spiritualist churches. I watched lots of so-called conspiracy theories during this time. They opened my eyes to what is going on in this world. What a shock. Then a Christian testimony popped up in my YouTube feed. I watched hours of them.

After two years in my room, it hit me... I needed to take part in life again. But I just could not find the enthusiasm. It was a massive struggle for me. I did not want to do anything or be with anyone. I spent two years looking for an anchor to get me back into the stream of life. Eventually, I started doing yoga again, together with practising shamanism (applying frog poison to burned skin, then vomiting violently), Chakra balancing, Mantra chanting and Qi Gong - I even intended to become a teacher. I had been on an Ayahuasca retreat in Spain as well, I was taking Valium and magic mushrooms (micro-dosing), and I had become very promiscuous dating and having with anyone I met.

No matter what I tried, nothing seemed to work. I felt depressed and empty. I was about to start micro-dosing on Acid tablets which were supposed to alleviate depression.

I was still watching Christian testimonies and wanted to know how people got God in their life. I had bought a Bible and gave up working on the Sabbath. Trying to find God, I went to a church service that said you could receive the Holy Spirit, but nothing happened.

Then in 2018, I found out that all this New Age stuff I was doing was demonic; it all went against God. I heard that everything I was doing was causing my depression and lethargy, and it broke me. My 'crutches' were gone. How could I do life without these crutches? At that moment, I knew for sure God was the Only Way. I broke down crying, begging God to come and get me. He did but differently. Two hours later 'The Last Reformation - The Beginning' movie popped up in my YouTube feed. Watching this film, I realised two things: that God was using those people, and that I wanted God to use me as well. I contacted someone from the movie straight away and got baptised just three days later, on June 30th, 2018.

A new life doing what Jesus did

My only crutch now is God, and I have never been happier. That emptiness, lethargy, and low-level depression is no longer there. God has changed me entirely and supernaturally. I have such peace now, and contentment. God is real, and He is using me. My life is now like The Last Reformation movie. But most importantly, I have a close relationship with God.

Call out to Jesus today. He will rescue you from your pain, your phobias, your addictions, your disease, your anxiety, depression, isolation, your confusion. You must cry out to Him and change your ways. Believe in, trust in, and follow Jesus, be baptised as an adult, and receive the Holy Spirit. Only then will you truly be set free and become a child of God. You will be able to have a personal relationship with God and get to spend eternity in Heaven with Him. Doing good deeds will not get you to Heaven, but Jesus will.

Jesus is the answer to everything that is wrong with you.

"Come to me, all you who are weary and burdened, and I will give you rest. - Mathew 11:28

RAJVIR – Powerful encounters, including a visit to Heaven

The Lord has been good to me in all the kindness he has shown me.

Born in 1998, I was raised in a Non-Christian household - Dad, Mum, my younger brother, and I. Growing up, if anybody asked me what religion I was, I would have said I was a Sikh. I would occasionally go to the temple, do a couple of religious events in the year, and wear the metal 'kara' on my arm.

I believed there was a God, but I had no personal relationship with him. I developed a routine of reciting a prayer to 'God' most nights before I went to bed, but I did not know what I was saying because it was in Punjabi.

That all changed in 2013.

Satanism in the Music Industry

I was 14 at the time; it was the Summer holidays. I was staying at my Grandmother's house, watching videos on YouTube. One day a video came up in my feed relating to Satanism in the Music Industry. After watching the video, I started watching more and more about this topic. It was interesting, and not something we think much about. Some of the music we love to listen to have some of the strangest video content, and we cannot make sense why. These videos I was watching were being made by Christians who were explaining the Satanic elements in the music.

These videos would usually end with a prayer someone could pray to accept Jesus into their life, at which point I would often move on to the next video. Eventually, after watching so many videos over a few days, I came to the reality of how strongly Satanism was promoted in these music videos. It was not a 'one-off' feature. I was scared.

What if it is all real? What if there are Heaven and Hell? There must have been a reason why these music videos were promoting Satan, and why do they go against Jesus? Why not oppose other religious faiths?

Jesus - better than the evil one

Being scared, I decided to find the prayer to accept Jesus into my heart. I went up to my room and whispered this prayer so that nobody else in the house would hear me. As soon as I finished praying, my head cleared up, and I was at peace. Fear was gone. I had never had this happen to me before.

Now I was at a crossroads because all my life I identified myself as a Sikh. I was not looking to abandon my Sikh faith, but equally, I could not deny what I had just experienced after praying to Jesus. I resorted to a test: I would pray to the Sikh God, then pray to the Christian God. What I found, was when I prayed to the Sikh God, nothing was happening. I was closing my eyes and talking to the ceiling. But when I prayed to the Christian God, The Heavenly Father, it was a completely different experience. My prayers were answered; something was happening; my Spirit was alive. It was unlike anything I had ever known in my life. God was real; he was listening to my prayers and answering them. He was my Heavenly Father, I was one of his children, and I was safe.

I was a secret believer in Jesus in my house for about one and a half years. My immediate family did not know about my faith in Jesus.

At that time, the Lord was so patient and kind to me. He was answering my prayers, and the Holy Spirit was with me; it was incredible.

Brother saw Heaven

Towards the end of 2014, I started thinking that I should share my faith with my parents. The problem I faced was fear. I had thoughts on how I would break the news to my dad, but God had other plans.

It was very soon after New Year; I was still on my Christmas half-term break. My brother and I were in our room, awake one night. I asked him if I could pray for him, and he allowed me to. He was lying in bed and closed his eyes. I put my hand on him and started praying, but I was praying in my mind.

As I was praying, I said to Jesus how my brother was someone who would believe things if he saw them, to which I asked the Lord Jesus to show my brother Heaven. A few moments later I tried to speak to my brother, and he responded, "Bro, don't disturb me, I'm seeing Heaven".

My heart filled with joy, hearing this, and I was crying. It had not even been ten minutes, and Jesus answered my prayer. It was incredible. My brother started describing what he saw in Heaven. Eventually, he told me what he could see God. He could not see God's face, but he described God as light, which is what we find in the Bible (Exodus 33:20 and 1 John 1:5). After that, he told me that he saw Jesus. He did not speak to Jesus verbally, but it was a telepathic communication.

Now my brother was not a Christian, he did not know who I was praying to, or what I was praying for, and he did not know what the Bible said about God, yet here he was stating specifically Christian details. After going to Heaven, my brother started crying, saying he had felt like he was the most special person in all the world. He was only ten years old at the time.

Within the next couple of nights, I asked him if he wanted to go to Heaven a second time. On that second night, my brother went to Heaven again. After going to Heaven a second time, my brother wanted to pray for me to go to Heaven. I accepted his offer; he put his hand on me and prayed for me. But nothing happened. It turns out he had prayed to the Sikh God, which is why nothing happened.

After persuading him to pray to Jesus, he prayed for me, and I started to feel very differently internally. I felt like I was falling, and I was so scared that I stopped my brother from praying. From then on, I went through a difficult time where I felt as if I was going to die. I was terrified. I had struggled to sleep and was incredibly fearful. It was during this time that I shared my belief in Jesus. Because of the worry they had for me at the time, they did not respond as strongly as they could have. My faith was not a priority for them at the time.

After nearly a month of struggling, I went to my room and prayed to God the Father about this issue. I prayed that if this was to do with my brother praying for me to go to Heaven, that I did not want to go to Heaven until the day I died, so when I enter, I never have to leave again. From that night on, there was a significant change, and I had such a peaceful night of sleep.

After that period of trouble, a new issue surfaced in the house. My parents wanted me to go back to being a Sikh, but I was not prepared to go back. I had seen Jesus do too much. To go back to my old religion just was not right, and it was not life. This conflict of interest was not without its arguing, anger, and disagreements. The difference in faith lasted for much of 2015.

It was not until the end of 2015 that my dad accepted Jesus into his life, and my mum believed in Jesus soon after. Since then, we have seen and heard the Lord doing miracles in our lives, and the lives of people around us.

After coming to Jesus, life has changed. I can walk into situations with God by my side. God can encourage me, answer prayers; it can be a real-life with him. There is so much I could share about how good Jesus has been to me, how much he has done. I know that God changed me for the better from where I was all those years ago. That is something God does; He changes us from the inside out. We are 'Sanctified' and, in the process, God cleans us and makes us better people. He fills us with his Holy Spirit and 'Sanctifies' us by his Holy Spirit.

God has been so gracious to us as a family, giving us with this testimony. He has been so kind and loving.

Now, this is eternal life: that they know you, the only true God, and Jesus Christ, whom you have sent.

John 17:3

JENNIFER - A broken life healed and restored. From New Age to Jesus.

Ever since I was little, I wanted to heal others. I loved to love and help people. I wanted to be a nurse but failed my maths.

At 19, I fell into what I thought was the loving arms of a medium who shared so much truth about my life that I believed I was directly communicating to God. He controlled my life. As I felt so uplifted by the experience, I convinced myself I had direct access to God via him, so I followed him and all his readings.

I was urged to live in Cyprus and stay in an abusive marriage. The enemy was destroying me through the demonic world.

I started to break the link and speak to God directly, but then I went to a Mind, Body, and Soul fair where a lady so graciously approached me and said I walked in with angels and she can heal me through reiki for free. Looking back, after this encounter I lost my home, job, and car, I lived in a refuge and ended up in a court system. It was terrifying. It is a wonder I am still here!

In October 2019, I went to London to deliver a public speech in Parliament Square on domestic abuse. I felt such heaviness as soon as I stepped off the train. Lots of people had mentioned the devil, but, in New Age, we never discuss this. I was intentionally not asked to speak, so I felt very betrayed.

Then I went to McDonald's with the group I was with, and a beautiful lady collapsed in front of me high on drugs, in her dressing gown. I watched others continue to eat their food as if she was not there. The paramedic asked her to wake up as people were eating, and I asked loudly "What type of society have we become where we can eat when a lady is dying before us". I wanted to hold her, heal her, and cleanse the ignorance of her pain, but I could not do anything.

Then I returned home and, soon after that, two beautiful people who, even though they have endured persecution, walk our Earth with such grace, forgiveness, and devotion to God and Jesus, both told me that New Age was demonic. So, they urged me to read the Bible.

Soon after that, my beautiful sister took me to York, and we stayed in a crisp white apartment. As my home was very colourful, when I returned I felt a massive need to paint my bedroom white and detach from crystals and all New Age paraphernalia.

A few days later, a beautiful lady sent me The Last Reformation movie. I watched it, repented, got baptised, and received the Holy Spirit.

All in a short time after I realised the devil deceived me into false teachings. Then I began healing on the streets through Jesus. Very rapid and never been so happy.

Changed from the inside out

My life has transformed entirely. Before the baptism, I could swear, and immediately after being saved God's Spirit in me rejected anything unholy. I have become a better person and a better parent. God has taken the thorns out of me, and Jesus has healed a lifetime of trauma.

I had Post-traumatic street disorder (PTSD) but got healed. My back was crumbling, but Jesus healed my back by aligning my legs as my right leg was shorter than the left leg.

33

Because today I have love and compassion, I want to heal the sick through Jesus on the streets of East Yorkshire for the rest of my years.

I am so grateful to know who God is and the Salvation Jesus brought to us through His sacrifice. The Holy Spirit guides me, and I am filled with love that bursts my heart open.

I stand in God's truth that the enemy is leading the New Age world – it is sugar-coated to look so inviting, and it attacks the kindest hearts. It is designed to keep you away from our Father God and Jesus.

The lost people matter to God. God saves us so we can assist Him with saving. He transforms us so we can change others - the broken matter to God.

Peter replied, "Repent and be baptised, every one of you, in the name of Jesus Christ for the forgiveness of your sins. And you will receive the gift of the Holy Spirit.

Acts 2:38

JEREMY – Rejected by his parents, accepted by God

The Early Years

My mum was single, and she had me after having an adulterous relationship with my father. I was the outcome of that relationship, and my father wanted a divorce from his wife (clearly unhappy in his marriage), but she would not play ball. My mum resigned to being on her own during the pregnancy and decided to have me and, presumably, bring me up. Unfortunately, she quickly realised she could not cope with being a single mother as in the early 1950s was taboo, so she put me into foster care for two years.

It became increasingly evident during that time that I was a troubled little boy, and social services decided that I needed the security of one home, so another family adopted me.

Everything was ok until they had another child, and, at seven years old, they sent me to a boarding school.

Rejection has always been a sensitive issue for me. We all need to be loved. People spend their lives looking for love, which is mostly confused with lust. The problem is perfect love is hard to find via a human being! I spent most of my life needing to be delivered from rejection, and little did I know that the solution was to be found in Jesus Christ.

My initial conversion was the fulfilment of seeking the meaning of life. Nothing tragic had happened in my life to motivate me to seek some comfort. Yes, I was carrying around my rejection which was affecting my relationships, but I did not have a clue how to solve that pain.

Life was ok, and I did not look for a crutch. I was married, earning decent money, owned a house, and had a beautiful daughter, and yet I knew there was more to life than what I had experienced so far.

I investigated different "religions" not expecting to find anything. And then in late 1986, I found the truth. I was invited by my brother in law to join him and his wife at church. I accepted his invitation, not expecting anything. It was at North Baddesley Baptist Church. My background was Church of England high church services, so a Baptist service was different and less formal. A visiting preacher was giving the sermon, and I cannot remember it, but he did talk about the cross and invited the listener to change their minds and believe in Jesus Christ as the Son of God and as their Saviour. I responded to that invitation thinking that this was what I had been looking for, though I had little understanding of what it meant. That morning I decided to follow Jesus and so started a long and at times challenging journey.

My conversion was not dramatic. No vision of Jesus. No tingling in my body. No falling. And yet I knew something had happened.

After Conversion

Despite my conversion, I had found the church service uncomfortable. Everyone seemed to know everyone, and this unsettled me. The rejection was rearing its ugly head. So, the following day I decided to find an Anglican Church to visit and pray to God asking Him what to do next. At the local church in Otterbourne, I knelt on the pew and prayed to God that He would show me the next step to take.

John 14:14 says this *"If you ask anything in my name, I will do it".* "In my name" is the key. The prayer needs to be found in His will and something that He has not already done for us.

Faithful to His Word, God answered my prayer, and within a month, I found myself at a house church, free from all the religious trappings generally associated with a high church. I knew at that moment that Chandlers Ford Christian Fellowship was to be my first spiritual home.

The later years

Since 1986 my journey with Jesus has been far from smooth. For twenty-five years after my conversion, I walked without the freedom Jesus had bought me on that wondrous cross, two thousand years ago.

I have now learned that what happened back in 1986 was that I was "born of the spirit". Our natural birth was "born of water", but I needed to be "born again", as taught in John chapter three. But what I had not understood was that back in late 1986 it was my Spirit that was a new creation. The old "me" had died on the cross, along with Jesus, and I was a new creation. I had understood that I was a new creation, but I was perplexed that my thinking did not change much, and my body certainly was not new.

Once I received proper teachings that I am Spirit (created in His image – God is Spirit) with a soul (mind, conscience, feelings, emotions, etc.), in a body, it all started to make sense. It was my Spirit that had been created new and was identical to Jesus; Jesus was now in me and me in Him. That sounds weird, I know, but it is true.

John 8:32 says that *"it's the truth you know (understand) that sets you free"*. I had spent twenty-five years as born-again Christian thinking I was a second-class believer because I did not understand what the Word of God was saying to me. That is why Father sent the Holy Spirit, after the ascension of Jesus Christ, to be our helper, our teacher, and our comforter. When you get baptised in the Holy Spirit, He comes and lives inside you. When you ask Him questions, He answers, and He also teaches you to understand what God's Word is saying. Without the Holy Spirit, you cannot understand Scripture.

Today, thirty fours years later, I am still learning to understand the truth. We will not know all things until the second coming of Jesus Christ, but with the Holy Spirit helping us, and teaching us, we are on the right road. For every individual, Jesus Christ is the only way to a relationship with our Heavenly Father, our Creator.

What I have learned is that God is good all the time; this is His nature. God loves us so much that He gave His begotten Son, that if we believe in Jesus Christ as the Son of God and as our Saviour, we will be saved. The Good News of Jesus Christ is not complicated. Jesus was punished instead of us, so God is no longer angry with us. Jesus is the bridge to a beautiful relationship with our Creator. The revelation of God's love for us is so important, as it releases us to love ourselves, and then love others. That is what I was looking for back in 1986 and have found in Jesus Christ. The rejection I suffered as a baby took many years to heal, and even today, the scars sometimes surface on a bad day when I momentarily forget what Jesus did for me. Those scars are healing though and have been replaced with a deeper understanding of God's love for me. That revelation of God's love comes when we understand God's Word and believe His many promises to us. Promises that He keeps. I am now secure in the knowledge that I have a Heavenly Father who loves me, accepts me, has forgiven me my sins, and most importantly forgotten them, and ONLY wants to bless me, not harm me, and to give me a hope and a future.

To the Jews who believed Him, Jesus said, "If you hold to my teaching, you are really my disciples. Then you will know the truth, and the truth will set you free". - John 8:31-32

ALEXANDRU - From doubting God to making disciples of Christ

I grew up in the church from the age of nine, and, over the years, I started to be more and more involved in the church. I was a leader in the children's program, then a leader in the youth program, and, as I became an adult, a worship leader. I finished two bible schools over four years and led some house church bible studies. Even though I was all the time in church and studied the Word of God, I must say that I had no personal relationship with God. I lived in sin. I led the worship with the pack of Marlboro cigarettes in my pocket, and I spent my nights partying with drunkenness and immorality. I knew ABOUT God but not I had no idea what it would be like to have a personal relationship with Him.

After many years of living in this cycle of sin combined with the church, I reached a point in my life where I said, "God does not exist!" Because I had never met him, I was tired of hearing from others their testimonies of how they met God, and their lives changed. I was very tired of listening to sermons, and I said to myself, "If you exist, I give you a week to prove to me that you exist. Otherwise, I will never come back to you again". And I want to tell you that God answered me in five days.

After five days a friend came to me and said, "Alex! Are you going to a seminar tomorrow? Someone will come and teach us how to make disciples and how to heal the sick. When I heard this, I thought: "Oh, not another seminar... " But that night I could not sleep much. I felt that I must go. The next day I went and sat back on the last chair. After about 10-20 minutes, for the first time, I felt the Holy Spirit coming over me, and I have no words to explain how I felt. I felt a warmth all over my body, and I felt love for me. A voice inside me said, "I am here". That was the day my life changed forever.

Today I walk in my redemption as I provoke others to stand up and have an active life sharing Jesus and His power with others. As a young man, I am determined to bring revival to this generation and beyond! Alex lives as you read in the Book of Acts. Healing the sick and telling people about Jesus is part of his daily life. Today he is leading a ministry called 'Let's make disciples'.

I have been crucified with Christ, and I no longer live, but Christ lives in me. The life I now live in the body, I live by faith in the Son of God, who loved me and gave himself for me. - Galatians 2:20

OLIVIA - Drug addiction led to demonic oppression

Even though I was born into a Christian family, my family life was very turbulent. My father loves Jesus, but my mother was not on the same page. She has severe mental health problems. My parents had a miserable marriage, and divorce was always on the cards since I could remember.

My father tried to hide from her attacks and rages, and so he threw himself into his work as a teacher with physically disabled children and later deaf education.

I grew up insecure, confused, and angry.

We went to church every Sunday, but it was more of a rule than anything else, and I found Christianity was legalistic. I rarely saw evidence of love and faith in our daily lives. It seemed more of a lot of rules than anything else.

I had never heard of grace when I was growing up, even though my father did family devotions as often as he could, teaching us the Bible... it seemed dead and lifeless.

At six years old, I do have a strong memory of my sister and me fighting and my father taking me upon his knee and telling me about Jesus. I remember him explaining that if I asked Jesus to come and live in my heart, He would help me not to fight with her. I wanted this so badly, and it was a moment I will never forget when I said this prayer.

My mother said she was a Christian, but I never saw her having a relationship with Jesus. She was often incredibly stressed, angry and violent towards us. She kept herself busy with three jobs every day, working till late and so we did not see too much of her, but when we did, it was hard.

I had a grandmother who loved Jesus. Even though she did not live close by, she bought me some Psalty praise tapes. As a child, I used to put them on in my room, and, as I sang along, I would feel this beautiful peace and sense of love fill my room.

At this point, I started talking to Jesus on my long walk home from school. I would find myself singing to Him and telling him everything. At age 9, I went to a holiday Christian day camp and here I was baptised in the Holy Spirit and began to talk in tongues.

My older sister and I got sent to boarding school when I was 11. I did not last long there. I felt so depressed that, at some point, I took an overdose of pills as a way of escaping from it all. I remember loving the sick feeling of being out of this world. I was floating around for days.

Destructive life in boarding school

I started high school in South Africa at age 13 as a day scholar, and, from here, my troubles began. Due to my insecurities, I desperately wanted to fit in. I began to try and join in with the popular groups and doing what they do. I started smoking and drinking and getting involved with boys.

A lot of the parties I went to were "free for all", and so I had to lie to my parents about where I was going knowing that my parents would never approve.

By age 15, my parents saw my decline, and they realised I was out of control. They could not control me or my actions any longer, so my mother decided I must go off to boarding school again. She did not want me at home any longer.

During my first six months of boarding school, I developed anorexia and stopped eating. I became very withdrawn. I had frequent nightmares every night of my mother beating me, and I slept walked most nights around the hostel, waking up in strange places on various nights.

Towards the end of my 16th year, I changed from being quiet and withdrawn to becoming the rebel and bad girl at school. Then started the next two years of bunking out of the hostel most weeknights, hanging out in clubs and bars, smoking dope, and drinking as much as I could whenever I could.

Eventually, the school hostel politely asked me to leave as they could not control me.

I did, however, manage to finish my A-level exams and, on the day of my last exam, my bags were packed and ready to hit the big world.

Dependent on drugs

I got a job as a waitress at a restaurant in a big city shortly after this. It was not long before the staff introduced me to the best clubs and designer drugs out there. And so, began my "high and wildlife" of drugs and partying, which continued for some years.

The drugs which started as just recreational soon became a necessity to survive each day.

Lots of boyfriends came and went. I lived here, there, and everywhere. My weight was dropping significantly. There were many crazy times when I know I should have died... My life was spinning out of control.

I got arrested for shoplifting, and I made a deal with God. I told Him if He would get me out of it, then I would come back to Him. He did bail me out, with no charges, and I kept my end of the deal. I went home and started furiously reading my Bible and going to church. And I experienced His love in such a beautiful way. I would spend long periods in prayer and fasting seeking Him. I was desperate for God. But the pain in my heart was still there, and it was not long before the drugs lured me back.

My mother was very controlling and wanted me to study and go back to the city that had been my downfall. I did not last long in the same city with the same old friends, so soon I went back to my old habits. But the drugs got heavier this time, and the highs got higher. My mental health was suffering too. I dropped out of the course I was studying.

I would have times of wanting to come to Jesus; I had dreams about Him. I heard Him calling me through songs on the radio. I felt Him pursuing me all the time with His love. In my darkest moments, I felt the Holy Spirit would rise in me, and I would start speaking in tongues. He was still with me. It was what seemed like backward and forward in my faith. But He never left me. I just could not seem to shake off my demons or the pain of the past.

I began to have very dark dreams, and they were telling me to leave behind the beliefs of my childhood. I believed they were right and began to explore other paths. I got involved with a lot of New Age people and found myself longing for the peace they claimed to have. I adopted their lifestyle for a season, but my heart was longing to connect with the Greatest Spirit in the Earth, the Maker of Heaven and Earth, the One who saw me in my womb, the One whose Son carried my sin, shame and pain. However, I still had the anger, the suffering and the rebellion from my past. I did not want to accept Jesus; I was fighting Him.

Then I had a dream I will never forget. I was meditating and began to levitate around the room, someone walked in and said the Name of Jesus, and I dropped like a stone to the floor. This dream repeated, and I knew quite plainly what it meant. But I still could not surrender and so continued more of the high life and all the mess that goes with it.

God sent her future husband to save her

Until one day I was working in a bar, and a man walked in. He ordered a drink, we chatted, and he took my number. I never thought anything more of it. He, on the other hand, was quite astonished that he recognised me from a dream he had had:

He was on his way to Dubai with a shiny new chef job in a top hotel, while I was continuing my wild life and running from Truth.

About eight months later, I was trapped in a very destructive relationship and the new drugs he introduced me to, meant that addiction had a very firm grip on me. To maintain such a heavy habit was costly, but it became my world. I struggled to relate to having a normal life like everyone else.

I was losing confidence in myself and became very introverted and fearful.

Then came a text message out of the blue from a number on my phone that said, "John Chef in Dubai". He became my lifeline.

At a time when I felt so alone and trapped in my destructive relationship and addiction, here was someone who believed in me.

My parents, who by this time divorced, had long since disowned me and I knew I was an outcast, but John spoke words of life to me in each text he sent. He encouraged me and helped me to have confidence again. Because of that, I was able to have the courage to move out and find my place. Now followed the loneliness, absolute loneliness. I knew God was there, but my life was a mess. I would ask John to pray for me on many occasions when I was out of control on a bender of chemicals. He did not know how to pray, but I just told him to ask Jesus to help me. And so, began John's journey of meeting Jesus.

It was in this time that I got on my knees on the floor in my flat and cried out to God: "God if You are real, will You show yourself to me and get me out of this mess?"

One day John phoned me, and he shared with me the vision he had for his life, and, for the first time in a long time, I felt a shaking of the Holy Spirit. His vision for his life was the same vision God had given me many years ago. I knew then that I had met my husband. But he was still in Dubai, and I just did not have the strength or ability to get out of the place I was in.

Tormented by demons

One night, after getting back from an underground party, I saw a picture of a group of witches sitting around a fire laughing and cackling. The noise of their mocking laughter was so loud in my ears, yet no one else could hear it. From that moment, constant voices started following me wherever I went. Day and night, they always mocked me, ridiculed me, laughed at me. They were destroying me, and I was full of fear. Everything I did, they watched me, and I became a wreck of nerves. I stopped wanting to go out anymore and could hardly leave the house. I was going crazy.

One day I visited an old friend at her parents' house where she was staying, and the strangest thing is that the voices remained behind the fence. They could not come into their property. For the first time in a long time, there was silence. In this family, they were all Christians. As soon as I walked outside, I could hear the voices on the fence again, but they could not come close when I was in their house.

Now I realised what these voices were, and I started to understand the big picture of what was going on. But still, I did not know how to extricate myself from the mess.

Saved by the grace of God

Eventually, John came back from Dubai and got a job at a Game Lodge/ Safari Park on the other side of South Africa. He invited me up for a week to visit him and, after the week, he asked if I would like to stay with him there and eventually get a job at the hotel.

I realised this was my opportunity to come clean and come back to Jesus. I had to take this opportunity even though I did not want to leave my life of sin.

Reluctantly, I left my life in the city behind me and began my journey of walking with Jesus again. It was not easy as the voices were still there, following my every move and thought, but I had got used to them. The fear was still there, as well. I had so many strong urges to go back to my old lifestyle, but God was having His way now.

I began reading the Bible, knowing that this what my Spirit needed; this was my key to freedom. It was the Word of God that fed me and sustained me in the coming months. I clung to God's Word to hold off my addictions. Without His Word, I was lost and empty. The more I read from the Bible, the more freedom I began to experience, the more peace I had in my heart.

I began to teach John the Bible every evening when he came home from work. We would sit up till late, with me teaching him all I knew from the Bible.

He was so hungry and was born again in a short time as Truth became a revelation for him.

I surrendered my life to Jesus afresh.

I baptised John in the bath one night, and, when he got out, our whole house was immersed in the tangible glory of God. It was so strong upon us and truly glorious that we could not speak. We will never forget this evening. God was right there in the room with us, and His Heavenly Hosts had filled the room. We were in awe of Him and were speechless in His Great, Holy, and Beautiful Presence.

Attacked by the devil and offered to worship Satan

The devil was angry; he was not happy at all that we turned to Jesus. We began to receive some strange dark, malicious emails. Someone hacked my phone and listened to my calls.

Satanists began to track my every move, following us around and playing sick pranks on us. They would turn off our electricity box outside the house at 9 pm every night and perform strange rituals around the house. We were terrified. We lived in constant fear of what they were going to do next. They broke into our home and smashed the music player so that we could no longer play worship music. When we left the lodge once a week to go to the local town, we would find strange people following us. It was so surreal.

I soon discovered that the people from my past, who were a syndicate which ran drugs, girls, bouncers, were actually Satanist based, and that is how they secured their power. I had never known this. Now they wanted me back.

They knew John as he had previously rescued girls from their syndicate and the reason He had to leave to Dubai was to escape their death threats. I had, unknowingly, got involved in these same circles. Now they wanted me back. They made some very generous offers to me – to be altar girl in their sacrifices and running the girls in their agencies. There were times when my phone would ring, and I would get recorded podcasts of Anton LaVey, the author of the Satanic Bible. My dreams were bizarre with confrontations between Christians and Satanists.

They did, however, fear me marrying John and seemed to think I was their possession and should return to them. They hated John; they wanted me alone. I remember we were driving along the motorway when a car came to run us off the road. It was the most terrifying experience I ever had, but, as we prayed and cried out to Jesus, we felt angels pushing us ahead of them, and we were able to escape.

The demons left

One day I was in our little house praying. The voices were so loud, and I had enough. I began to pray in tongues, and the tongues grew in authority. I felt a righteous anger rise in me against their mockery and control of me. I felt Jesus' authority in me for the first time since coming back to Christ. The tongues grew louder, and the Holy Spirit more powerful. Suddenly, I heard some loud, high-pitched screaming going off into the distance, getting softer and softer as I continued praying until they were gone and there was, finally, peace and silence.

I knew John wanted to marry me, but I was resisting it. For a long time, though, I was hearing the Holy Spirit telling me that this was my husband. Finally, I could no longer resist the voice of God. I asked him to marry me on Valentine's Day of that leap year, and, four days later, we made a covenant with God and with each other and got married.

We vowed to give our lives for Him and the glory of His Name and to use our union to extend His Kingdom and fulfil the vision God gave to both of us many years before.

The satanic syndicate knew immediately about what we did, and they knew they lost the battle. Shortly after this, we had official documents signed at a local home affairs office.

A new beginning

The peace I felt was incredible. The fear was gone, and I had such hope for the future. I felt joy deep inside my heart, and I knew the Maker of Heaven and Earth loves me. His love gave me a reason to live, to sing, and to surrender my whole life to Him. His Spirit in me made me feel alive. I was a new person as I chose to leave the old behind and embrace the new. I felt like finally my feet were planted on the rock, and I was unshakeable and immovable. I was Jesus' beloved, and He was mine. And so, began our journey of walking with Jesus and finding freedom as we fixed our eyes on Him daily.

Therefore, if anyone is in Christ, the new creation has come. The old has gone, the new is here!

2 Corinthians 5:17

PATRICIA – Healed physically and emotionally after an abusive marriage

I grew up in Colombia; raised in a Catholic family without a Bible at home, where the name of God was professed without really knowing him deeply. I have seen much superficial religiosity and empty life in the Catholic Church. I started to have a genuine relationship with Jesus when I stopped all resistance and opened my heart. After completely surrendering to Him, I came out of the prison in which I was living. After I confessed each of my sins directly to Jesus and sincerely commenced loving Him, I could see His mighty power working in me. He began to bring healing in all areas of my life.

Revelation 3:20, *"Here I am! I stand at the door and knock. If anyone hears my voice and opens the door, I will come in and eat with that person, and they with me"*, came true and alive for me in 2014. Jesus was at the door knocking wanting to have dinner with me, and I welcomed him.

I had autoimmune disease derived from Lupus, and I remember that one day I could not get out of bed. My dear sister Andrea prayed for me and spoke to me about Jesus Christ. I remember that the first miracle that the Lord did was to give me the peace that surpasses all understanding. I believed in Him with all my strength, knowing that I would rise from anything. Soon after my sister prayed for me, the Lord healed my autoimmune disorder. All praise to God!

Years later, I realised it happened as it is said in Acts 16:31, *"Believe in the Lord Jesus, and you will be saved - you and your household."*. My sister turned to Jesus ten years earlier than me, and today my entire family believes in Jesus and got saved after they have seen my life changing for the better. I have become like a child who believes everything and knows that what comes from Father will be genuine and fulfilling. God made great miracles in my life where I experienced healings, and I could see his power over me.

Eyesight restored

I have experienced many of God's miracles in my life that I am grateful for, but I would like to share how my eyesight was restored in 2016. For me, this was the turning point when I realised that God is real. By profession, I am a civil engineer. My eyesight got damaged after being overexposed to the dust and sun most of the time. The epithelial membrane was torn, and no doctors could help me. Without any hope from the doctors, I turned to God for help. I prayed and believed that the Lord would restore my eyesight. Then, one day, God listened to my request, and I felt the healing happening in my eyes. I knew this was happening because I felt as if someone put stitches in my eyes. The next day I went to see my doctor, and I told him about my experience of stitches. He examined my eyes, and he found that I had a scar which was in the process of healing called cicatrisation. As a result of this experience, my eyesight was completely restored. That was the moment when I realised the King's power and understood you could receive healing for yourself and heal others too.

Rescued from an abusive marriage

I was married to an Italian man who had problems with excessive alcohol and drug abuse. We lived a stormy life. Though it was harsh and painful, I was able to forgive my ex-husband. In his alcohol and drugs madness, he was always very abusive with me, and I suffered a lot on account of a toxic relationship.

One day, I could not stand it anymore, and we separated. It was not easy for me, but God was there to raise me up. It was difficult because, on one side, there was all the pain of the loss of having a company and, on the other hand, the hope to know that there are new opportunities and that with God every day is a new beginning.

I had to move on. God healed me of all the bad that I could have done, and I no longer needed to take extreme measures to end my life. For the time I stayed in this toxic marriage, I harboured suicidal thoughts because I could not see any way out. But God empowered and freed me from the strong clutches.

Back on track

Now I am on the right track. I am happy, calm, patient, and I have found infinite peace. I am alone with God waiting for the right person who He has for me. I trust Him.

I was in a trial period in the desert for forty years until He made me demolish the fortresses that had imprisoned me and go to the other side of Jordan breaking off all the shackles and living freely with, in and through Jesus every day.

Today I can proclaim God's eternal life because I have seen it with my eyes, and my hands witnessing the power of God. I know that my Father wanted to make me testify his miraculous works to encourage others to believe that Jesus can save and restore lives. I will never be silent in proclaiming that God is the King of Glory -The Creator and Jehovah with vast Armies.

Today, as His committed disciple and an active part of the army of God, His Holy Spirit runs through my veins stimulating every aspect of my being.

The love that He first gave me is ever alive so that his Gospel may be spread, preached, and proclaimed throughout the world in every language without ceasing.

God took me out of an abusive marriage, healed me, and gave me a new life. You can have your miracle too! Genuinely believe in Jesus and see what amazing things He will do for you.

We love because he first loved us.

1 John 4:19

JAHIR - Jesus gave him freedom and power

My name used to be Jahir Islam, but Gold told me to change to Israel, so I did it what He said.

I was a devout Muslim throughout my life. Every day from the age of 5, I went to mosque learning Arabic, Quranic recitation, and additionally attended Islamic school of Quranic memorisation – I was training to be hafiz. I memorised about half of the Quran from the age of 12 - 15. It was always my dream to go to Heaven and work my way up to the best level and obedient Muslim I could be.

62

I kept away from all forms of evil, including smoking, drinking, women, and so forth, and I would always pray extra in addition to the five daily prayers. My parents noticed my strong desire into being an Islamic Scholar and Hafiz and felt quite concerned and uncomfortable as my focus swayed away from my education (specifically GCSE's). Because of this, they decided to end my Islamic career. From that point, I was quite depressed but swiftly shifted my focus to school, career, ambition and performed well in academics and then went on to go to London to study Mathematics at degree level for four years.

At the university, I longed to make good Muslim friends, and unfortunately, all Muslims who I associated with were lukewarm. All were frustrated to see how strong and disciplined in Islam teaching I was and would bully me and make a mockery. So, I left those group friends. Soon after that, I started to associate with non-Muslims, and hang around with them till the end of year 2. They also made fun of Islam. It was a nightmare.

For a few months, I had a YouTube channel to teach others how to become a good Muslim, highlighting the importance of taking the religion seriously. My family thought I was too extreme. Everyone in Wales was gossiping about me, so without having any support, I got discouraged and stopped doing it. After that, I joined the Islamic society at university and pushed myself to get involved with them and be part of their prayers, talks, and lectures. My new Muslim friends were worldly and completely neglected every form of Islamic advice I would give to help them.

My Christian friend

I have got my first job at a call centre where I stayed for ten months at least. My manager was great. At the time he was a very worldly person, intellectual and scientific, coming from a Hindu background but an atheistic in his belief. He left the company halfway, and out of nowhere, I bumped into him months later, talked to him, built a relationship personally. When he then told me he is now a Christian, I was concerned, furious, and sad. We became friends. I would visit him and vice versa and talk about our life and also religion; I tried hard to prove to him tawhid via Quranic scriptures and why it is the truth, and he kept mentioning about his relationship with Jesus and the Gospel. I could not convince him, but, deep inside, I was convicted and drawn to what he had. My heart was crying out for God in a relational way, so in prayer, I told Allah that I want to know him relationally and hear him. I told him that I will give him a break and that he cannot punish me.

My friend invited me to churches, and I went out of respect. Then I realised I was wrong in my fixated view of Christianity (which was Catholicism). I saw people falling, manifesting, healing, worshipping from their hearts. I thought this is a cult and it is demonic. Again, he invited me to a church, and I went for him, but this time I felt something in my heart – it was very peaceful, but, because of my pride, I could not reveal it. This church held a home cell at my university to meet Christians and talk. I went along, and I joined worship but neglected the name Jesus when singing. However, while there once again, I felt something in my heart.

Later, I had so much pain in my tooth, and as I told them, they immediately start laying hands on me and commanding healing, and I got healed. I was astonished but still thinking this is demonic!

He kept calling me about going to church, and I was so frustrated by his insistence and blocked him from reaching out to me for months. One day I suddenly bumped into him again, in early 2017, and, while he was on the phone, he was telling his sister that I am in his prayer list and that he is praying for me daily. Since then, we became close friends.

My secret girlfriend

During that time, in 2015, I met my first girlfriend, a Polish girl at university. Being an Islam, I was against this in the beginning, but as I became more liberal and open to non-Muslims and various cultures, I started having deep conversations with her and fell in love. I entered a relationship which lasted for more than 3.5 years. I tried converting her to Islam and wanted to marry her, but it did not work. I did everything in my strength and realised my words have no power because she was far from considering Islam. She was from a Catholic background but was very spiritual of the New Age religion and was trying to convince me to have the same beliefs. I was curious.

During our relationship, I would visit my parents often but hide my relationship from them. I did it for the whole of 3.5 years. I knew there would have been severe consequences if they would have found out.

Fast-forwarding to three years after graduating and getting a job, I decided to visit and catch up with my family during a weekend in December 2017 – I never thought that weekend would be the change and transformation of my life!

The truth will set you free

On the weekend of 9th-10th December 2017, I went to visit my parents. At some point, my girlfriend was calling me, so my mum became suspicious. I was faltering and went to my room. While we were talking on the phone, I heard a movement underneath my door and suspected it was mum listening. So, I started to pretend that I was talking to a guy friend, but near the end of our conversation, I could not resist but say "I love you" and ended the call. Smash! My mum opened the door and cried out "Do you have a girlfriend? Who is this girl?"

I lied and just said "it's not a girl, just a guy friend", but she refused to believe me and kept asking. I lied once more and said, "ok, it is a girl but just a friend talking about a project".

Then, my mum said, "Please Jahir, tell me. We will not do anything bad. Don't lie! We're open to hearing what you have to say".

Never in my life have I heard the voice of God but, at that moment, I was silent, and suddenly I heard an authoritative, powerful voice over my ear saying, "TELL THE TRUTH".

I was confused though, and I thought I was insane, but I knew it was a good thing, so I just spat out the truth and said "yes mum, I do have a girlfriend. I love her, and I want to marry her. Please give her a chance. She will come to Islam gradually!"

I pleaded not to call my dad as he was an aggressive and short-tempered man, but she called him. I had to avoid any form of trouble, so I told my mum to leave and locked my door.

All I could hear was him verbally abusing my mum, swearing, yelling the rooftops, and accusing her. As time went on, my parents consulted all family members about this and then called an imam to perform an exorcism on me and check if there is anything wrong in me. They found nothing. In the morning, my younger sister called me to go downstairs as my dad requested.

Being hot-tempered, he gave me an ultimatum straight away. He said, "Jahir you have two choices – either to leave the girl, your job/university, London, everything there, come under this roof and never go back there again or to leave us, you are no longer our son, we cut you off from our bloodline from this day on and if we die no one is going to tell you. You have a decision to make within 2-3 hours and, if not, then I will force you out the house".

I tried negotiating, but he would not accept, so I just cried and rushed upstairs for help by calling my best Muslim friends, but none were willing to support or help but instead just said: "it's your life, you're an adult, we have problems, sorry". I understood but panicked and relied on my one Christian friend who was previously my work manager. I knew he was passionate about God, loving and friendly, so I told him about my situation. Straight away, he started telling me about Jesus. He said that He loves me, He died on the cross for me, and He wants a relationship with me. My friend said that Jesus is real and He can save me. I was fuming because I had enough of listening to this, so I muted the phone and screamed: "Jesus isn't the son of God. He's just a prophet!"

Feeling guilty for what I did, I unmuted him, and he said to me the words that pierced my heart - he said "Jahir whether you believe it or no, it's the TRUTH! Do you want to know who God is and have a relationship?" And I said "Yes", and he said "you have to cry out and ask him with all your heart, and He will reveal himself to you" and I replied saying "you're right I have nothing to lose; it's not going to cost me anything, I want to know God!", so we ended the call there.

I went down on my knees and cried out with all my heart and uttered: "Allah I don't believe in you anymore but GOD I know you are real, just like my friend. JESUS, if you are the way, the truth and the life, show me right now, show me in a dream that you are my LORD and Saviour and my GOD and only then I will accept you, otherwise forget it!" then I went on to challenge and say "GOD I'm going to go to bed now (it was only 11:30 am/12 pm) and I want to see you".

Supernatural encounters with Jesus

So I did, and right away, I fell in a deep sleep. I saw myself in a dark place, with only Muslims in an airport (some Muslim country perhaps) and out of nowhere a Muslim gang of boys were chasing me with weapons and eventually got me down and beat me. I became paralysed, could not even scream while people were walking past me without any care, and I could only whisper "someone help me".

A sudden bright light shunned from the night sky and hit me - I got instantly healed. I was scared, and I started to have doubts in my mind "this can't be Jesus, this isn't Jesus". I looked up, and I saw a large human body figure, a long white raiment, long brown hair; from the face, all I can see was a powerful blinding light.

As a Muslim, I never read the Bible before, but I heard these words, He spoke:

"YOUR FAMILY WILL FORSAKE YOU BUT I NEVER WILL, I AM JESUS CHRIST YOUR FATHER, AND YOU ARE MY SON, I SHED MY BLOOD FOR YOU ALL. EVERYONE KNOWS ABOUT ME, BUT THEY DONT KNOW WHO I AM. BELIEVE IN ME, AND I WILL BE WITH YOU FOREVER, THAT'S HOW MUCH I LOVE YOU JAHIR!"

I woke up and felt so much peace, however, I started to rub my eyes to clear them, and all I could see was darkness although it was afternoon. I realised at that point that I lost my sight. I was completely blind. I was panicking crying, screaming, but no one could hear me. Out of nowhere, I heard the voice of God audibly, and light came passed my eyes - I got healed, and my vision got restored! Hallelujah JESUS.

After all of that, I still did not believe in Jesus and had too much fear to leave Islam, thinking I will go to hell. That day was a Sunday. My uncle came later and tried convincing me to stay and not move, but I made my decision to stay with my girlfriend. They asked me to leave the family home if I made that decision, so I left my parents' house.

While on the couch, my Christian friend called me and told me to go to Golder's green station and join him at a house church where he was. He told me to let him know once I have arrived at the station. When I arrived at the station, I realised that my battery was dead. No one was willing to help me, and with no charge, I asked God, in my heart, to make a way, and amazingly my phone came back restored with a call from my friend. He called an uber for me, and then it died again, but it was what I needed to get to the house church.

Once I reached the house, I felt a sense of immense peace. I explained my story and they were supportive, emotional, and affectionate. I was amazed. They advised me and then asked to pray for me, I was gaining strength and peace, and finally, they asked me "Do you want to accept Jesus Christ as your Lord and Saviour and repent from all your sins?" I paused for a while, so fearful, but suddenly the yoke broke, and I accepted Jesus into my heart and repented. Peace just flowed through my body when I did this.

Demons left, and a new life began

A week or two later, I came again, and, while everyone was praying, I heard tongues and was so weirded out and scared. While others left, some of them asked me if I want to speak in tongues and receive the Holy Spirit. I was hesitant but then accepted. They prayed intensely, and my leg started to shake aggressively as a demon was leaving me (it was uncontrollable). It became more and more intense, and I began to praise God as the Holy Spirit entered and flowed from my belly upwards out of my mouth, and I spoke in tongues.

Finally got baptized two weeks later and became a new creation. From the photo they took, we witnessed the light of God shining from my face and knew, with confidence, that the God I serve know is the true living God. Thank you, Jesus. Hallelujah to the Kings of Kings.

Today, Jahir is following Jesus and making disciples as he shares the gospel, healing the sick and teaches new believers what he knows.

Keep your lives free from the love of money and be
content with what you have, because God has said,

> *"Never will I leave you;*
> *never will I forsake you."*

STEVEN – Attracted by the light, after a tumultuous life

When I was around five years old, my mum and dad divorced, and, to this day, I am not sure exactly why. Dad, at the time, was an assistant minister of a church in Wood Green, London. Mum remarried when I was around 7, and I grew up in more of an atheistic household. I was interested in knowledge, philosophy mostly, and I was dismissive of faith and the existence of God, mainly believing this could have been what had caused my parents' marriage to break up.

When I reached the age of 13, I smoked my first cannabis joint and first started drinking at 14. As I reached my late teens, I was stoned on weed almost every day, using cocaine, pills, LSD, and often getting drunk. It was my way of escaping the world. It may have looked like I was happy, but inside I was lonely, had no real purpose, meaning, or direction in life. I was going from one job to another without being able to keep one.

One night, in my mid 20's, I had a dream, and in the dream, I met this being - although I could not define His features, His face was radiant. Life and light itself were just flowing out of Him. As I woke that morning, I felt tears of joy and love; it was indescribable and overwhelming. I knew it my heart that this being was Jesus. Despite having this experience, I continued abusing drugs and did not want to stop.

At around 27 I met my girlfriend Rachel, now my wife. She did not know too much about my bad habits. One day she said, "I'd like to go to church", as she was from a Catholic background. But was not born again. Shortly after this a stranger approached me in the street and said, "You need to go to church". I replied, "No, I don't, but my partner does". So, I advised Rachel about this, and she ended up going with a friend.

Attracted by the light

That night Rachel went to church, and, as usual, I was stoned, but as she returned, I noticed something had changed. She was radiant, glowing, and then I understood that on that day, she was filled with The Holy Spirit. The darkness in me reacted, and I became jealous. I said, "You need to choose God or me". With little hesitation, Rachel looked at me and said, "There's no comparison". It was a big slap in the face to my pride and ego. I soon began to understand I knew nothing about faith.

As time went on, I began to seek evidence of God's existence. My first recalled prayer was "God if you exist, please show yourself to me". He did it in so many ways. One of the ways was through the Bible, which I read almost cover to cover. Although I did not fully understand its contents, it became clear to me that it was more real than anything I had ever studied.

On the 8th of February 2008, I decided to give my life entirely to Jesus. Privately I told God I would give him my whole life. Publicly I repented, turned away from my old life and sin. At that moment, I experienced The Holy Spirit filling me and was overwhelmed with peace. It was like a dam broke, that been building up inside of me. I had broken every one of the ten commandments. Nobody told me, but I knew, in my heart, that I was forgiven. I got baptised, and the old Steve had to die. Since this day, my life was filled with joy, purpose, meaning. God has been transforming me, and many people from my past have said I have changed so much. God has done many great things in my life. Physical healing, miracles, people set free from demons. I have witnessed thousands of people responding to the gospel. Hundreds becoming born again. God is also using me to disciple others. He has shown me His love, and I can never go back. I have seen too much.

He died for all, that those who live should live no longer for themselves, but for Him who died for them and rose again.

2 Corinthians 5:15

BOSE – Second chance after a severe car accident

I was once in the world, but I give Glory to God for counting me worthy to be His child (1 John 3:1).

My dad passed unto glory several years ago, and I lived with my mum and siblings from a young age. My mum would take myself and my siblings to church on Sundays, and I thought going to church was a compulsory part of life. I started learning about Jesus in the children's church, but although I had an idea about the story of Jesus, I did not fully know why this was so important to me.

My mum would talk about the importance of ethical behaviour and all the things parents would generally advise their children to do to be good children and become responsible adults. My mum was a good example, and, naturally, children grow up copying the behaviour of those around them. But it was not good enough only to be good.

I got into secondary school, known as the high school in some parts of the world, and I had a lot of friends. Upon completing my secondary education, I went into university. During this time, I realised that accepting Jesus Christ ties in one way or the other to how I live my life and where I spend eternity.

I had left home as my university was a few hours drive from home. There, I found myself always longing to attend church on Sundays - this was normal to me growing up – as the Bible says *"Please do not forsake the gathering of the righteous, it is important for growth"* (Hebrews 10:24 -25).

I was going to church, but I still did not give my life to Christ. At that time, I attended parties and was in relationships that did not glorify God. I was living my life like everyone else, while I continued going to church regularly. There was a desire for God, but I did not know how to get close to Him.

Looking for God, I went for crusades, Christian fellowships, and religious gatherings of all sorts alone, but I was still not a devoted child of God, there was something still missing. I wished I would grow up to be a pastor, but it was just a wish then.

I found myself always giving my life to Christ whenever I had this opportunity, but not following up to live the life of total submission to God. Though I tried to be good and felt a sense of self-righteousness, there was no quality connection with the almighty God, and I did not feel full.

Wake-up call

The year 2000 was the beginning of my journey towards knowing God truly. One night, I was involved in a road traffic accident coming back from a club party.

The interesting thing was that I did not believe a lot of 'men of God' in those days, especially those that were saying that they see visions. I had been given a warning message not to attend any party in the coming weeks because, if I would attend, the outcome will not be favourable. I said okay to the man of God, but I did not listen. I said within me - I will go for the party and then prove to my mum that vision seeing was not a thing to believe always.

I did not know what had happened immediately after the accident because I almost died. I went into a coma, and I remember waking up several hours later at the hospital with my mum and elder sister beside me. I had bandages and lots of stitches on my head, shaven head, a cervical collar, and severe pain. From this experience, I learned that there is indeed a thin line between life and death – because I would have been dead on March 11, 2000. I also realised the words from God should not be ignored irrespective of the messenger - you either accept the message or reject it prayerfully.

During recovery, I noticed people went about their daily lives, and some would sympathize with me while it took me several months to recover. I realized that I was alone and did not need to please anyone but God. My family was incredibly supportive, especially my mum, who never blamed me for being disobedient. I realized that God had given me a second chance, and I certainly did not want to misuse this opportunity.

Soon after the car accident, I fainted because of me not eating while being on medication, so I found myself in the hospital again.

Following my recovery, I continued my journey of trying to be that Christian that had a great relationship with God. There were lots of distractions back home in Africa. I had a good job, but somehow, I had the desire to leave the country for a while, so I travelled to the UK to study. Still, I did not know God fully, nor did I accept him fully as I was studying, working, shopping and just going on with life casually not acknowledging God.

However, the experience of the road traffic accident in the year 2000 remained with me, and I think this made me always want to have a personal relationship with God, knowing that He gave me another chance to live right. I believed God wanted to save me.

God wants us to have a good relationship with him, but sometimes we ignore him.

I joined a church in North London sometime around 2007 and decided to join the workforce – this was when I got a clear understanding of how to have and nurture a good relationship with God. I served in the church as an usher, and we had several meetings - these meetings combined with church services, listening and reading the Word of God, desiring more of God, helped me grow in Christ.

I will not say I know the exact day I gave my life to Christ because I gave my life to Christ several times but still found myself living a carefree life not acknowledging God but what I know is that God saved me. I can say I am now in a great relationship with my Father and Saviour.

One thing to note is that being a child of God does not make you immune to challenges, but you will know that through it all, God is with you and He will bring you to your expected end which is always good.

When I lost my sister in 2016, I wondered if God loved me, but, through the grace of God, I was able to let go. I believe my sister is in a better place.

A few things I learned from my sister's passing.

1.   Death is not final like most people say – It is a transition.

2.   Death is part of living, and if Christ tarries, we will all have to return to him through death, so we must prepare for the other side of eternity.

3.   The Holy Spirit Comforts us.

There will be tribulations, but it will all end in praise. Trust God.

Please do not think that you have made a mistake or two, and God no longer loves you. Continue in this journey to seek God. You will grow as a Christian, and you will be glad you did.

A new life

Please view my experiences of before vs after Christ below. There are many examples, but I will just share the list below:

Before Christ:

1. I lived in fear;

2. I did not know what tomorrow had in store for me;

3. I harboured hatred and anger to some people;

4. I did not care about other people's feelings;

5. I would revenge and be happy to revenge;

6. I just wanted to be a winner even if I was not doing things right;

7. I desired to fit into society at all cost;

8. I was somewhat proud and thought my achievements were my doing;

9. I made a lot of wrong decisions by myself;

10. I doubted that Jesus is real.

After I met Christ and with the help of God

1. I no longer live in fear;

2. I live by faith and God has been faithful. I know my tomorrow will be fine;

3. I harbour no hatred and intentionally control my anger. I also continually check myself carefully not to enter the trap of anger;

4. I now care about people and genuinely love people;

5. I do not look to revenge;

6. I try to live holy as God is holy;

7. I no longer strive to fit into society. Pleasing God and winning souls for him is more important to me. He loved me first and continues to love me;

8. I now know that promotion is from God, and He provides all I need according to his riches in Glory. Without Christ, I can do nothing.

9. God guides me even when I think I have made a wrong decision; all things work out for my good.

10. I have a personal relationship with the Almighty, and I know God is real. You need that personal relationship with God to avoid doubts.

Please give your life to Jesus Christ, feed on the Word of God, grow in this journey, and win souls to Christ. God is real, and there is absolutely no gain in sin. Start your relationship with God today, and enjoy the journey. God bless you.

If we claim to be without sin, we deceive ourselves, and the truth is not in us.

I John 1:8

LUCILLE – Death and grief is not the end

My journey of faith in the Lord Jesus Christ began in 1992 when friends took me to a Spirit-filled church. There I heard for the first time that I needed to believe in Jesus Christ and receive Him as my Saviour for the forgiveness from all my past wrongs so that my relationship with God, the Father can be restored.

I have always believed in God, the maker of the Universe and people through my Catholic upbringing. Because of that connection with the church, I thought I was automatically Christian. I believed God was up in heaven, and He is ever correcting me for my sins, and I must do different things to be accepted by Him. He was a very distant father in heaven.

Something happened in my heart one day in that church which was quite different from what I was used to, and it completely changed the course of my life. I had an encounter with the living God when I heard the good news that God wanted a personal relationship with me, and this relationship came through accepting salvation (forgiveness, healing, deliverance) through Jesus, who had already paid the price so I could be reconciled to Father God. I said yes to that invitation, and a divine exchange took place at that moment. I felt an incredible peace and a sense of coming home. I felt all guilt and shame removed from my life; my burdens were taken off. I felt light.

Overcoming grief after daughter died

A little bit about my life up to this point: when I found Jesus, I was a single parent of a special needs 8-year-old beautiful girl called Stephanie. There was a lot of guilt in having her out of wedlock. Therefore, to know on the inside that I had been forgiven from all my past brought freedom into my life.

I have never looked back since but been in a pursuit to know this God and Saviour who thought I was worth dying for because of His great love for me.

In my continued journey with the living God, I have discovered that He is a God who cares about the little things and the big things in my life and the lives of those around me. I have found that He is faithful to His promises to provide, to heal, deliver, and comfort.

I had "random" acts of kindness like having the electrical wiring of my whole house for free just when I was figuring out the budget for it, holidays paid for even when I was able to pay for myself, to name but a few.

In the healing arena, I have been completely healed from gynaecological related pain that I have had for over 20 years, and I was able to stop taking pain medication.

I have prayed for other people over many years, Christians and non-Christians, and saw Jesus heal them from sciatica and other joint pains. I have also seen liver tumours decreased in size, so no operation needed, a crooked, broken bone being restored years after an injury and many more. I also witness to God calming the weather so a family member could travel by sea for emergency treatment.

I have discovered He is a real God who could be trusted to do what He says He will do and that He is a God of miracles.

He is a God of comfort and hope as I found out when my daughter died to go back to her Father in heaven. It was so reassuring when I met with her Paediatrician to discuss her post-mortem results as she died peacefully in her sleep. There was no cause of death but only her diagnoses. The Paediatrician said to me after I told I was a Christian that some people just leave this life and they (the doctors) do not know why. That was what she believed happened to Stephanie, just confirming what I knew in my heart and so it brought comfort and hope to me know that it was "see you later, mum".

A little bit about the influence Stephanie had in her 13 years on the earth: when she died, I received cards from so many people who knew her but not known to me, expressing the blessing she was in their lives: her spirituality, her smile, and how she brought joy. She was a child who could not see, speak, was entirely dependent on all her daily needs, and had learning difficulties through brain damage from a cardiac arrest a few days after she was born.

I discovered through her life that while your earthly tent may be damaged, your spirit is not, and the latter can still respond to God. She loved being in the presence of God, loved worship, and being in prayer meetings.

I became fully aware of her connection to God after she died, through the impact she had on the people around her. I met those people for the first time at her funeral. God became God of comfort and hope in the next few years of adjusting to life without her. My faith grew stronger and stronger through this.

Never too late

How can you not love a God who loved you so much that He gave His only Son to save you! His love is unconditional, and it is the same love He puts in the heart of everyone who put their trust in Him, so we can all bring the message of hope and healing to everyone through love. To that end, when I took early retirement from my National Health Service, I had time to get to know God to a higher and new level.

I have just completed two years at the Eastgate School of Supernatural Life and saw my life transformed through a deeper connection with Almighty God and more profound love and compassion to see people encounter Him and His goodness for themselves. This course facilitated this as it is designed for students to know their true identity in Christ, intimacy with God and then impact the world around them with His love and goodness, which involved moving in the gifts of the Holy Spirit.

When you invest time and money to know God, He does not disappoint. Knowing in your heart and mind you are a daughter or son of the King of kings makes you royalty and hearing from God is your birth-right is life-transforming.

I have learned to be His daughter first and then to serve Him out of that. This brings true freedom and joy to serve Him with gladness.

As a Christian, expect God to speak to you for yourself and others. He does this in so many ways - through His Word the Bible, vision, dreams, prophetic words, an impression in your spirit, and even through nature to name but a few.

I am still on a journey to know (understand and experience) this amazing, Almighty God and Father, and this will always be the case even beyond this life.

There is victory when you follow Jesus as He has already overcome the world and death. There is only life and light in Him. My quest and hunger to draw closer to Him grew stronger and stronger because there is no greater love to be found except the unconditional, unfailing love of God that is available to every one human person on the planet.

Your best service to God will come out of that close relationship with Him, and there will ease because it will be supernatural as it is God's power enabling you to do what you are here to do. This will always involve others getting blessed by what you bring from the heart of God.

You will keep in perfect peace those whose minds are steadfast because they trust in you. Trust in the Lord forever, for the Lord, the Lord himself is the Rock eternal".

Isaiah 26:3-4

NALEDI – Loved, forgiven and blessed

Looking back, I can see that God has always had me in the palm of his hand and been looking out for me.

My father was diagnosed as a paranoid schizophrenic, and my mother was an alcoholic. They were never unkind to me, but I did not come from what you would call a healthy family. God gave me a loving grandmother who I adored and spent a lot of time with and also gave me a best friend who came into my life when I was three and is still my best friend to this day. I spent a lot of time there, so they became my surrogate family.

I have always believed in God and attended the local C of E church with my mum but did not understand who God was, or Jesus and I certainly did not realise that I could have a relationship with Jesus.

One day when I was around 12, one of my friends invited me to church. It was a charismatic bible believing church, and as soon as I set foot in the Church, the Holy Spirit touched me, and I could not stop crying. I did not know what was happening; all I knew was I felt peace and love.

I carried on going to church till I was around 15, but then the pull of underage drinking and partying took hold, and I did not go back to church until I was 21. My life was in a bit of mess, and I had lost my peace.

I became involved in the church and started to sing in the worship team. I made friends in the house group, but it was not long until I started getting into inappropriate relationships and going back to my party ways. I was still dipping in and out of the church. I left the worship team and the house group and began to pull away from my Christian friends.

I met my now-husband at work and eventually we got married. He was not a Christian, but he never stopped me from going to church.

Miracle baby girl

I tried to get pregnant for five years, and nothing happened. We had various tests, and there was nothing biologically wrong with either of us. It was a mystery why we could not conceive.

I was getting very depressed, and I remember saying to God, "if you bless me with a child, I will give her back to you". I eventually got pregnant with medical intervention, and my beautiful miracle baby girl was born.

I started attending a little home church, and that is where my faith began to grow, and I learned more about who Jesus was, that He loved me, that I was precious to Him, that He was my Father and He wanted good things for me.

I remember I was in the kitchen one day, and I heard God telling me that he was going to restore what the Enemy had taken from me. At the time, I did not understand what it meant, and I filed it away in the back of mind.

A word from God announced the way

I had moved on from the little house church as my daughter needed to be in Sunday school with other children and one day we had a guest speaker come to visit us and during the sermon, he looked directly at me and asked me to go to the front of the church. He said that he had a word from God for me and told me that I was going to be an influencer to my friends and particularly to my husband. Two weeks later, my daughter nagged my husband to come to church which he did, and he enjoyed it and kept coming back. He eventually committed and became a Christian.

My husband used to play bass and acoustic guitar, but he had not picked up an instrument in years. After he became Christian, something in him made him yearn to play again. He mentioned to our pastor in conversation that he could play the guitar, and he joined the worship team.

We are both now involved in the music team, I lead worship, and my husband plays the guitar.

It is incredible what God has done for me, and He has restored what was stolen from me in my early walk with Him. I used to think in my youth that going out to the party was much more fun than going to church and praying, but the opposite is true.

If you spend time with Jesus, just listening to His voice and letting Him guide you in life, it is far more interesting, fun, and fulfilling than any night out ever will be!

To know the love and peace of God is something so precious and beautiful, and to know that whatever storm you are going through in life, we have a big God who is there to hold you, love you, and guide you is the best feeling in the world.

For I know the plans I have for you," declares the Lord, "plans to prosper you and not to harm you, plans to give you hope and a future. Then you will call on me and come and pray to me, and I will listen to you. You will seek me and find me when you seek me with all your heart.

Jeremiah 29:11-13

GABRIELLE – Jesus destroyed the works of the devil

For most of my life, I have been plagued by paranormal activity, starting as a young child. The shadows were not just shadows; they were genuine manifestations of evil coming right up to my face.

My parents played Ouija board game when I was around nine and, by doing this, they opened a pathway to the demons straight to their daughter without them knowing.

As I grew up, it became part of me, and I did not give it much thought. But once my firstborn arrived on the scene, the activity happened more frequently and it became terrifying to the point that my child was being threatened. Things happened at night and in broad daylight. I have never been able to watch horror movies because it is too close to home, and it brings back memories that I would rather forget.

The spirit world is real, and it has two sides - the bad and the good.

Freedom in Christ

At the age of 37, I joined the right side after God set me up to believe in Jesus. I resisted God for many years, but He knew to get my attention He would have to remove me from my busy life. So, He took me on holiday to another country where, unbeknownst to me, the owner of the holiday home was a bold, energised, Pentecostal female minister. Exactly what was needed as I was a tough nut to crack. I received the full-on package of sermons and prayer for two weeks in-between sightseeing and having a good time.

Each day more was revealed to me about who God was and how much He loved me.

The day before I flew back home, I gave my heart to the Lord and was immediately slain in the Spirit. All the heaviness I had been carrying for many years was instantly removed. My life changed forever.

God taught me how to clear all the demonic activity out of my life. After I became a Christian, I learned how to use the power of Jesus Christ against evil spirits by praying and declaring the name of Jesus Christ. It worked, and since then, I have never had another experience of paranormal activity.

Evil spirits are real and can destroy your life. Only God can remove them. I regularly thank Him for protecting my family and me and for giving us the wisdom to live our lives according to the teachings of the bible.

Miraculous healing

My second child was miraculously healed from having severe bow legs (she had been referred to a specialist to see what they could do for her). As a teenager, she experienced God's power doing a bit of extra work on them. God is real.

Better life with Jesus

Before becoming a Christian, I was an atheist, not through choice, but because I grew up in an environment where God was not welcome. For me, the church was just the tradition of performing christenings, weddings, and funerals. At school, religious education was as dull as history (I love history now), so that did not have any effect on me.

My lifestyle was one of going to parties and getting smashed.

As I got to know God, I calmed down significantly and learned that partying was not all that life had to offer. I became a more considerate person and learned how to forgive all those who had done wrong against me. It was not easy, but with time my heart was at peace. The past was left behind me.

There is no Christian who is perfect. I am not perfect, but my life is enriched. I have a relationship with God, who loves me and protects me.

By faith, we understand that the universe was formed at God's command so that what is seen was not made out of what was visible.

Hebrews 11:3

VIVIANA – From a broken family to a life with a purpose

When I was about 22 years old, I felt very down mentally and spiritually because I realised I did not know how to love. I was worried how am I going to succeed in my relationship with my boyfriend at that time, how am I going to make it through this, when I do not know how to love. I did not know what love is.

I grew up in a broken family, where all I received were complaints and physical abuse. My mum bit me so bad one time that I ended up in the hospital. My parents came from broken families, and this is what they carried with them into their new family. The best decision I took was giving my life to Jesus at 16 years old. Now, looking back, I see that whenever I walked away from God, He came after me and brought me back on the right path.

My journey was not easy. I experienced a lot of anger and abuse when I grew up, and this influenced the way I lived my life until I turned to God and found love.

Two generations of broken families

I did not grow up in a Christian home, and my parents did not know God at all. At the age of 14, my mum ran away from an alcoholic dad and a very abusive environment. Soon after that, she met my dad and got pregnant with my brother when she was 15. They got married, and they stayed together up to this day. Years later she reconciled with her parents.

My nan (my mother's mum) was always involved with witchcraft. I remember she used to heal people with these supernatural powers. My grandad was an alcoholic who abused and molested all his children and grandchildren, including myself.

My dad grew up on the streets, and he did not have a mum or a dad. He had to work to survive and had his first job when he was eight years old in a bakery. He did not know how a normal family should be.

It was difficult growing up in a family with two broken people - a mother who had a traumatic experience with her dad and a father who did not have a mum or a dad near him.

I have an older and a younger brother and a sister who is ten years younger than me.

Physically abused by mum

Coming from a broken family, my mum did not know how to handle situations. She had an anger issue. I grew up with an overly aggressive, violent mum, who abused me physically and mentally. My mum did not know how to explain things to us; all she knew was to beat us up with everything she had up to the point of bleeding.

Growing up like this was very scary. I did not understand why my mum was so angry and always beating us up, and I did not understand why my dad did not say anything about it. I remember one day I asked my mum to help me with homework, and I ended up in the hospital. She took her shoe off and hit me on the head so hard that it broke and bleed. After that, she made me lie about it because she did not want people to know.

This was everyday life for me. Growing up with an angry mum was terrible hard. My dad never hit us but did not protect us either. He provided for the family but never showed any positive words or love to his children. He was there in the house, without saying anything to us – no 'hello', no 'Happy birthday', absolutely nothing.

My mum physically abused me for years, and so my older brother. This is all I know about my childhood.

The situation between my mum and dad was not good either. My dad was jealous, and my mum always had this temper. They were always fighting in the house.

I remember one day my dad sat my brothers and me at the dinner table and asked us who we want to live with because they decided to split up. I was so angry with what was going on that I said with no one "I don't want to go with any of you".

Hope in God

Around that time, God was working behind the scenes. My aunty Stella started to go to a local church and, knowing the problems at my house, she asked her pastor to come to our home. I remember this pastor because he had an accent. He was not from Argentina; I think he was from Brazil. He came to our house and prayed for my mum. Something happened at that moment because she started crying. Things began to change after that to the point that my parents did not divorce anymore. They stayed together and soon after that my mum got pregnant with my sister.

We all started to go to church, and things were ok for a little while, but then my mum turned away from God and stopped going to church. I continued going to church, to teenagers' meetings, and youth conferences.

During this time, the abuse continued not only from my mum but from my older brother as well; he always found reasons to bit me up. I cannot blame him for anything; this is all he knew since this was the family environment; he grew up in this.

In all that time, I was holding on to Romans 12:17-19 – *"Do not repay anyone evil for evil. Be careful to do what is right in the eyes of everyone. If it is possible, as far as it depends on you, live at peace with everyone. Do not take revenge, my dear friends, but leave room for God's wrath, for it is written: "It is mine to avenge; I will repay," says the Lord"*. I always remembered this verse, and I was saying to myself "No matter what people do to me and how much abuse I receive from people, I am going to leave it in the hands of God. I will let God handle this". I did not want to do anything bad and upset God.

Over the years, I continued going to church, and, when I was 16, I decided to get baptised and give my life to Jesus. I did not understand what I was doing, or how is it going to be, but I knew I had to do it. I remember it was very disappointing because no one from my family came. It was just God and me.

After I got baptised, I run to look myself in the mirror to see if something changed in me physically. Nothing changed physically, but I knew I made the right decision at the time. Something changed on the inside.

My life after the baptism continued to be challenging. The situation in my house was the same, and the abuse continued. One time my mum bit me up so bad that I wanted to leave home.

When I was 18 someone gave me the opportunity to go to work in England. I did not know much about it, but I made a crazy decision to accept it. Looking back, I see that God removed me from the hopeless situation I was in that moment. God did things in my life without me realising. He will do the same for you. He will change circumstances or remove you from the situation you are in to help you. Deep down, God knew my mum was not going to change anytime soon, my dad either. God had a good plan for my life that He needed to take me away from my broken and abusive family.

Lost in a foreign country

When I came to England, I was like a lost sheep. I was lost and lonely. I felt like a big wall hit me. I found myself in a foreign country, not knowing anyone, not knowing the language, working long hours for little money. I had no friends, no family, and the worse moment was that I did not receive any support from anyone back home.

One day I met a guy in Staines who knew Spanish, and he invited me to his church. I went there on and off. I realised that God did not stay there in Argentina, He came with me, but I did not have a close relationship with Him.

Because I decided to turn my back on God when I was 20, this made me make bad decisions and make mistakes which I still regret. I thought I could do whatever I want here in England. No one was watching me.

I did what I wanted, but this did not make me happy. I was feeling depressed, and I was struggling with relationships and friendships in general. I was struggling mentally, and, without God, my life continued going down the hill.

A year later, I met the man who later became my husband, but this did not help because I did not know how to love him.

Grateful to be a mum

After six years of being in England, I went back to Argentina, but this time I did now go back on my own the way I came. I went back with the man who became my husband. We decided to get married and have a child. When I had my son, I felt like something changed. I felt like God gave me this amazing boy exactly how I wanted. I was grateful for this, and in return, I thought I should turn back to Him. In 2011, when my son was six months old, I went back to church. I promised God "I am going back to church, and I am going to serve you. I don't care if my dad or mum gets mad". The church was very well organised and had some fantastic groups to support their members. There I felt loved by others, and I made some great friends. After staying in Argentina for three years, due to various circumstances, we decided to go back to England.

When we came back to England, the reality was different. I did not have a church, and I did not have any group of Christian friends who would pray for me and support me. For years I was looking for different churches seeking what I had back in Argentina, and I could not find here. I wanted the same presence, the same group of friends, the same thing that I had before. No matter where I looked, I could not find it here.

Back into depression

Back to England, I felt going down the hill again. I remember being in a church, feeling that I do not belong here. I did not find my place. I was going to church, but instead of feeling better, I was feeling worse. I had problems in my marriage, and we were doing worse than ever. I felt like nothing was changing, and I was not growing in any way. I felt stuck. We were drowning as a family.

I always had that conviction that if God is there, it has to be a change. If God is present, your life cannot be the same. I was desperate to live, but my husband did not want to live. The problems were too big for us to handle. I went to a different church, but it was the same. I continued feeling I was drowning; I could not do another day. I did not feel I wanted to wake up anymore; I felt mentally and physically tired. I could not do it anymore. This was at the beginning of 2017.

At that time, all I wanted was to disappear, to run away. I did not care about my home and my kids anymore. All I wanted was not to wake up anymore. I felt frustrated because I was struggling, even though I believed in God. I was wondering how people that do not know God do life. I did not see the point of living.

The Holy Spirit unlocked the potential

I remember one day I was on the phone with a friend who recently moved away, and she asked me a question that changed my life - "Have you received the Holy Spirit?". I did not want to answer because I did not have a clue what was she talking about.

Until that point, I did not think about the Holy Spirit. For me, it was God and Jesus. I never paid attention to the Holy Spirit until that moment. When she asked me, I said, "I don't know". After that call, for about a week, she sent me video teachings daily about the Holy Spirit. She asked me to watch them and promised she is going to call me the next Saturday to talk about this. I listened to them, and the more I listened, the more confused I got. I thought "There is no way I could receive that gift. I don't have enough faith. I am not worthy. I do not deserve it. I don't understand".

Next Saturday I was at home, and when I saw my phone ringing, I said to myself "Oh, no. There she is. What am I going to say to her? Do I have to lie? What am

I going to say?". She explained to me more about the Holy Spirit, and then she asked me if I want to receive the Holy Spirit. Straight away, I thought "Oh, no. She is one of those crazy people. Now I will have to lie and pretend that I wanted to receive the Holy Spirit just to make her feel better". This is what I was thinking to myself when she asked me that question.

I will never forget that the minute she prayed for me, I felt like something overpowered me. I felt heavy in my own body and felt there was a strong power over me. I was not in control anymore. I was crying out so badly. Straight away, I started to see things differently. I felt like I was a blind person who was living life in darkness and suddenly I began to see that now life has colours. I saw that there was a war between the flesh and the spirit. I started to understand what was going on. The word 'holy' made sense now. Holy Spirit had a shape now. At that moment I had a voice in my head saying, "I am with you, I am with you". Without realising, I heard that voice all over my life since I was a child to this day saying, "I am with you, I am here".

I was not the same person after that Saturday afternoon of 27th July 2017. My life changed completely at the moment I received the Holy Spirit. Everything became real. There was no religion anymore. This time I wanted to go back to church on Sunday because I needed it. Jesus became real. I started to understand and see God as a Father and that He is love. I began to fall in love with God. It was so overwhelming. I was so hungry, and I wanted more and more of this Holy Spirit, of His presence. I started going to conferences because I wanted more of God's presence.

I believe Jesus came to restore his people - I am one of them. He is restoring my life, and He is putting all the pieces back together. He gave me a new heart and a new purpose. Today I am no longer alone. I am loved. I do not care what is happening around me because I know God is there with me. There are still some things I struggle with, or I do not understand entirely, but I know that if he is there with me nothing and no one can be against me. No matter what I face in life, I always hold on to Mathew 24:13 – *"the one who stands firm to the end will be saved"*.

Lost but now found

All I want now is for people to know Jesus, to experience His love. Before I realised what Jesus did for me, and I received the Holy Spirit, I did not know what love is. Growing in a broken family with an abusive mum who did not know how to love was not easy. We are working on our relationship to this day. I learned a few years ago to accept my family and love them the way they are. I cannot change people, but I believe God can. He can change my family. I pray for mercy for my family, and I know I am going to see them giving their lives to Jesus. They do not realise how much they need Him, but I know this. I will keep praying for my family.

My deepest desire is for people to know Jesus because in the minute they know Jesus, they will know love, hope, peace and have everything they need. It breaks my heart when I see many people out there, even in my workplace, that have been abandoned, who never had a father, who have been neglected by their mums, abused by their parents, and they do life without Jesus. I was one of them before, and I was utterly lost. I was struggling in every area of my life and marriage because when you do not have God, you are empty, but when Jesus comes into your life, everything changes. This is my primary purpose – for people to know God.

Love may come in different shape, but for me, the genuine unconditional love came from Jesus. When you meet Jesus, you meet true love.

If you have the same problem as I had and you do not know how to love, turn to Jesus. Every day when I go to work, I pray "Jesus, I want to be more like you. I want to love people as you do and if I have to close my mouth, I will do it". I want people to see something of Jesus in my life. I want people to ask me "What is different to you" or "What can I do to have what you have".

I do not have much, but I have the best thing anyone can have – I have Salvation, I have Jesus in my life. I do not have to worry about tomorrow because Jesus is in it. He is always with me wherever I go. He was there in my worse moments; He is now, and He will be in my future.

I have no worries now that I have the Holy Spirit inside of me that helps me every day to be a better mum and wife. He provides for me in different ways. I cannot even describe how faithful He is.

God has a better plan

I do not know where I would be today without Jesus. I want to emphasise 1 Corinthians 2:9 because this will highlight my story and my experience since the minute I encountered God to this day - *no eye has seen, no ear has heard, and no human mind has imaged the things God has prepared for those who love him"*. This touched

114

my heart because God did so many things for me, things I did not even ask for. I came from a broken home, an abusing home, was sexually abused, growing up with anger, but God had better plans for me. I hold on, and I keep believing that there is a better plan for me. What the devil intended for worse, God is going to transform it into a blessing.

God has so many amazing plans for me because I choose one day to give my life to Jesus. I made that decision when I was 16. I got baptised and gave my life to Jesus. Then the day I received the Holy Spirit changed my relationship with God and with the world. I believe that these decisions changed the whole future of my life. My children will not have to struggle with the things I struggled in the past because God made everything new. I am holding on to this promise that God prepared great things for those who love Him. Jesus continues working in me, my marriage, and my family. He gave me a purpose and is guiding at every step. I went back to finish my studies and gave me new dreams and hope for the future. I received His love, and I learnt how to love my husband and my children.

But the one who stands firm to the end will be saved.

Matthew 24:13

CHRISTOPHER – A cry for help changed his destiny

I grew up in a non-Christian home and did not know Jesus. At a young age, my parents got a divorce, and this affected me badly. After this, I ended up becoming rebellious and causing trouble at school. I left school with disappointing grades and failed at college.

I started work at 18, but unfortunately, more money led to spending it on alcohol and cigarettes. This started as fun but soon began to control my life. As the addictions grew worse and worse, I also began to gamble and had other ungodly habits. The devil was controlling my life, but I did not know it. One time I heard voices which made me realise the battle was real, but I still did not change. I ended up progressively getting worse and not knowing where to turn. I developed depression and had a poor self-image. I thought that nobody loved me.

At the age of 24, I made a terrible mistake and, through a casual relationship, I thought I had caught HIV. I was scared and just wanted to run away and hide. I started to get sick and believed my life was over. In a moment of desperation, I cried out to the Lord while in the shower. I got on my knees and cried, begging for help. I said, "Lord, I know I've ignored you my whole life, but if you help me out of this mess, I promise I will follow you my whole life". As soon as I prayed that prayer, I felt all the heaviness leave and peace come into my life. I heard I voice inside saying "go to church, find some believers and get baptised". I ended up doing just that, and soon after I noticed that I did not swear anymore (which was a miracle in itself). I did not want to smoke any cigarette or drink alcohol, I did not want to gamble, and I paid back any unauthorised debt. I left my ungodly relationship and commuted to following the Lord. I was set free by Jesus Christ and given a brand-new life. I also had two HIV tests which came back clear, and I believe the Lord healed me. I received the baptism of the Holy Spirit at the age of 25, and since that moment, I have been in Christian ministry and have seen many healed by God's power and devils cast out. The Lord has given me a beautiful, godly wife and an amazing daughter.

Turn to God while there is still time, people. He will not let you down.

Trust in the Lord with all your heart and lean not on your own understanding; in all your ways submit to him, and he will make your paths straight. - Proverbs 3:5-6

ROY – Against God after being abused by Roman Catholic priests

Each time my wife urged me to turn to Jesus, I laughed, mocked, and ridiculed her stupidity. She could always expect a fight and tirade of abuse. Yet, she prayed for me almost every day. Most of the days, she was up at 5 am praying on her knees to Jesus, asking Him to save me. I could not understand what she was on about, because I did not believe in Jesus.

Whenever my wife asked me to join anything to do with 'Christian' I generally refused most of the time saying they are hypocrites, money makers, child abusers, molesters, rapists, and what part I have with them. Still, I was attending churches and doing religion.

Many times I retorted: why are these American Mega pastors asking us to pay when they travel in luxury jets? Why didn't Pope did not do anything during World War 2? Why did European people who call themselves 'civilized' and myself 'uncivilised' as an Asian, sent millions of Jews to the incinerator? Why are you trying to persuade me to be a 'Christian', I am already a 'Christian'? Why can't people love each other, rather than judging each other? If your God is real, why such anarchy, poverty, and indifference in the world today? What is the point of Jesus? What is the difference between Christians and any other religious group? They are all the same! Why are you talking about hell and trying to scare me? Why can't you just leave me alone!!!!

There were the questions I was telling my wife when she was talking to me about Jesus and Christianity.

Raped and abused

I had a pretty bad experience with the Roman Catholic church. At the age of 7 I was gang-raped in the churchyard by so-called 'Christians' and went on to be molested and abused by Roman Catholic priests, and others for few more years, and I hated it. At that time, I was asking where God was in all these? Religion had failed me entirely.

All this time, I measured who God was, is, and is to come by the actions and behaviour of others. I never sought God for myself and never read the Bible to find God and what God is saying.

Answer to prayer

My wife could not stop talking about Jesus, and I hated her for her consistent insistence. For 17 years she prayed for me, waking up at 5 am most of the days, seeking God on her knees. He answered her prayers on the 20th September 2014 at 11:30 am when Jesus spoke to me. The rest is history as they say.

The God I met was anything but what I heard from other people. He is a loving God, who wants to save us from sin and hell and is willing to give a new life; eternal life. God proved to me many promises in the Bible, including visions and dreams, healings, and the power of His Word over Satanists, witch doctors, and freemasons who were rolling on the floor at the name of Jesus.

I experienced what the Bible says when I put my pride and arrogance aside by ditching the old Roy with all the titles and let go of my views, opinions, and experiences and started to seek God. It was amazing. My mind could not get it when Jesus spoke to me in visions in broad daylight and through dreams, gave me a new language to communicate with Him, asked me to get baptised for the right reasons, and led me by His spirit.

Many people have experienced healing at the mention of the name Jesus, and many, many demons have been cast out from people in Jesus's name.

You can meet the same Jesus today!

Each time I mention hell, people say I bring fear, not love. But it is the love that will take the fear away, and it is the love of Sangeeta and God who took me out of hell; in eternity. It is a choice we have to make. Seek God for yourself.

God has done everything for you. Now it is your turn to receive the Kingdom of God. What matters most is what you will have to answer to Jesus on the day of Judgement.

Why don't you take a step today, just in case 1% of what I say is true? Find out if there is anything 'good' about the Good News of Jesus. It is a choice everyone has to make. The choice is yours.

But small is the gate and narrow the road that leads to life, and only a few find it.

Matthew 7:14

JAMIE – Saved from drugs and gangs

I was brought up as a Christian; my parents attended a big church in Bracknell, but I disliked church for multiple reasons:

- I found it very boring.

- I could not relate to it as a young man. The activities felt slightly too middle class and proper. I wanted adventure and wildness.

- My mum and dad did not have a good relationship. I saw them as hypocrites (praising in the morning and arguing in the afternoon).

My mum and dad's relationship affected me as a young man. I was also very insecure, sensitive, bookish, and impressionable.

Trying to fit in

I was bullied at secondary school and struggled to fit in. I then decided to become one of the "tough" kids. I hid myself, losing my identity for about five years. I hid my love for books and rebelled at school. I spent most of my school years outside the classroom or playing truant. I was often high on drugs in school, and I continued to become angrier and angrier. I continued to drink, take drugs, steal, and get into fights.

I left school with minimal qualifications despite having a sharp mind. My mum and dad got divorced soon after I finished school. It was a massive relief for me but also tricky for my brothers and me. At the same time, I felt guilty because I thought (rightly or wrongly) that it was my fault due to my behaviour.

I began the process of change slowly. I managed to go to university and became more confident. However, during my first year, I felt incredibly lonely at university. I began to get severely depressed and felt an emptiness in my soul. I contemplated taking my own life.

God had a plan

That year I was back from university for New Year's Eve. I had nowhere to go as I had severed contact with many of my school friends. My mum's friend Janine (who was a genuine and faith-filled Christian) realised that I was at home alone and asked her daughter to invite me to her party.

The party was unremarkable (having no alcohol or likely hookups), but I met two incredibly special people that night. Their names were Liam and Rory. I saw instantly that there was something different about them. I realised that they were Christians, and then I started to contemplate the Christian faith despite my previous misgivings.

I began to attend church every Sunday with my mum and little brother. A few weeks in, I gave my life to Christ, and my life changed forever. I was discipled by Rory for many years and served in his church and went to mission trips with him.

Eventually, I moved to Kerith to do a Bible Course and met my wife, Marija. We then served the church for four years and then were part of a team that planted a church in Egham/Hythe, where we continue to serve there today.

Therefore, if anyone is in Christ, the new creation has come. The old has gone, the new is here!

2 Corinthians 5:17

PETE – Disability was not the end. Stronger with Jesus

My Names Pete I am currently 51. I grew up a pretty standard child in the '70s until I reached the age of 8 when I had a severe stroke. I was rushed to hospital where I was put into a controlled coma due to the damage I had on the brain. I was in that situation for over eight months. During that time, the doctors told my parents that I might not be able to talk or look after myself, meaning that I may need 24-hour care.

When I woke up out of the coma, I quickly understood what my situation was, and I felt let down. It was like my life was over! I locked myself away in my bedroom, not wanting to see anyone for about a month or so. If it wasn't for my mum coming into my room one day to shake away the depression I was in, I think the doctors would have been right that may not have been able to talk or look after myself and that I may need 24-hour care. I remember my mum came on that day and gave me a bit of tough love by saying 'if you cannot be bothered with yourself then myself and your father will leave you to get on with it!'. Then they walked out of my room. I was shocked that if I would not have my mum and dad who would I have?

That day my life started to change. I left my room and went out to start a fresh new life. Well, that was what I thought.

My teenage years at school were tough; as a disabled person, I did not fit in - my mum fraught tooth and nail for me to be able to have a normal life. I was in the Scout movement, and I managed to go to a mainstream school. All these seemed to sound good but most of my early life, right up to the age of 30, I was bullied both mentally and physically which left me at times, again, totally isolated, and alone.

Lavish life

Fast forward to my mid-twenties, I am married, my job was a record producer and DJ, and my life seemed very carefree. I was living a very affluent lifestyle driving beautiful cars, living in a large house, travelling around the world, and, while away, I was staying in the best hotels. Money was never an issue. On the outside, it looked like I had everything, but throughout this time I felt something was missing. I never seemed to be happy.

This was the moment when things started to change - my wife left me, I lost my house, and I began to hit rock bottom. It was not until my best mate Steve was taken into hospital with kidney failure that I started to think that there was more to life than what I had experienced.

One step closer to God

While visiting Steve in hospital, I kept being asked by different people 'had I ever thought of going to church?' The church was not a place I thought I needed to be.

Steve spent his final days in the hospital, and I remember the last visit I did was, for some reason, very rushed. His mum left me to say goodbye, but I think she knew something I did not know. When I said, "I'll be popping in to see you tomorrow", he looked at me with a piercing stare and shook his head. I thought this was strange but flippantly agreed with him.

The following morning, I had had a call from his mother saying he had passed away during the night.

Now, at that point, my world was suddenly filled with questions - How did Steve know he was going to die? Why are we on this earth? Is there more to life than just this?

I spoke at Steve's Funeral, and Psalm 121 was used. It is a verse that I have never forgotten:

I lift up my eyes to the mountains—

where does my help come from?

My help comes from the LORD,

the Maker of heaven and earth.

He will not let your foot slip—

he who watches over you will not slumber;

indeed, he who watches over Israel

will neither slumber nor sleep.

The LORD watches over you—

the LORD is your shade at your right hand;

the sun will not harm you by day,

nor the moon by night.

The LORD will keep you from all harm—

he will watch over your life;

the LORD will watch over your coming and going

both now and forevermore.

Again, at the funeral, someone else asked me if I have thought of going to church. This time I am thinking 'yes, why not'. I attended a couple of churches, and I said that this was not for me; they all seemed so judgemental, and they did not want to listen to what I had to say. Things changed when I went to a church in a small church in Windlesham in Surrey. I went there with one of the people who had been asking me about God and attending a church. While at this service, the lay reader called Tony was giving the sermon, and it was what seemed to be remarkably familiar to my life. At the end of his message, he asked the congregation 'Does this ring true to any of us, if so please stand up'. I looked around the church thinking 'if I stand, will I be the only one?'. I thought I did not want that to be me. Looking around, I saw several people standing, and I felt a nudge to stand up. While I was standing, I realised I was the only one standing in the church! For me, that was my first step into becoming a Christian.

I was then invited round to Tony's house, and there, for the first time, I was accepted for who I am, I did not receive any judgemental questions. I was loved!!

I continued attending the church and gave my life to Christ. They found out I am a trained sound engineer, and since they needed help, I started working on the Tech desk. Soon after, the bass player of the worship band, who is a member of a Christian punk rock band called "Cephas", asked me to join them as their sound guy. I started touring with them, and, at some point, they asked me if I would join them in their ministry. I liked the idea, but it meant not being paid and stepping out in faith. I explained that I had only been a Christian for three months, and I had a mortgage, job, etc. Then I remembered the Psalm from the funeral, so I took the step, and I became their full-time Sound Engineer.

Stepping out in faith toward his destiny

During the three years the Lord provided payment of my mortgage, I received a better car, and He provided in many other ways. While I was with the band, we saw many people come to faith and saw God at work in many parts of our ministry.

While on tour, Andy, the bass player had a dream – he said I would meet a lady called Cathy while are touring. But what was even stranger was when he said that she would be wearing a red T-shirt.

Over the three years with the band, we had seen a lot of answers to prayers, but this seemed impossible!!

For months whenever we were playing at gigs, and I saw a lady in a red t-shirt I would ask if her name was Cathy but, disappointingly, it was not.

I did not find my Cathy in red t-shirt until the final year before that band disbanded, when we were asked to play a charity gig near our hometown of Camberley, Surrey. It was in a town that I have never really wanted to go to. That town was Aldershot Hants - there is where I met with a Cathy, but she was not wearing a red t-shirt. We played the gig, and I spoke with her for ages to the point the band was getting annoyed. We left, but she had impacted my life that night.

I prayed to see her again because I knew I had a full diary with Church events the next day, as I had now started preaching as a lay reader at my church. But one by one they all get cancelled. Next thing I know, I am back at this venue for the final day of this charity gig. Cathy is there in a Red T-shirt. We chat and became close over the next few weeks. A year later we got married, and the following year my beautiful daughter was born.

Living for God

I sit here writing this and again looking at Psalm 121. I can see the moment I decided I wanted Christ in my life, and, since then, I have never felt alone or empty, and my foot has never slipped. I found the missing piece, and that was Jesus.

I have been a Christian for over 20 years now. I now run a ministry called Alder Valley Revival where we put together training schools into bringing "God's love into Action" by encouraging people to step out into the streets and shine God's light and love into people's lives.

STEPHEN – God cares about your business

I always wanted to believe in God and noticed that people who were Christians had something – they had joy; they had life in them. They had something I have not seen in other people.

My grandma was in the Salvation Army, and my mum and dad met there. They got married and did not continue in the faith. When I was young, I did not go to church and did not know God.

God answers to prayers relating to business

I went through my life up to my 40s and had a business with eight people working for me. My business was going through some difficulties because of some government changes they were doing to the NHS. It just happened at that time that I had a phone call from a business coach who offered me a free consultation to see if he could do an evaluation of my business and perhaps direct me in a more fruitful future. I had a meeting with him, and we soon became friends.

We had weekly meetings, and he helped me decide to give up the NHS work and to go all private. This meant we had to buy a new property to serve the business better and be more presentable for when you have patients coming down to be able to cater and offer excellent customer service.

We found a new building that needed to be refurbished and needed a change of use from office to industrial so that we could buy it. We made an offer subject to planning permission. We got all the plans ready to divide into two separate units so we can rent one and use one. I was told that it would take about eight weeks to receive the planning permission. The sellers were happy to wait, and they understood I could not buy it without the usage worked out.

I handed my notice where I was working and through all the applications and the design process. It got delayed many times, and I spent about £5,000 trying to get everything together. After 15 weeks, the seller was getting angry that I had not managed to exchange contracts on the building. They warned me if I do not get it done by that Friday they had another buyer lined up who is going to buy the building for a lot more than I offered so that I would lose the property.

I had a meeting with the business coach, who was a Christian guy, on a Tuesday, and he said to me that something or someone was preventing me from buying this property. He said, "With your permission, I would like to pray for you". We were in the middle of the pub when he offered to pray for me. I said, "Sure, pray for me". He thanked God that He is our provider and told him that we would need an answer by Friday. He was very bold, and I remember saying that he can't talk to God like that, but he told me that when you pray you should believe that you have received, then you shall have it.

On Thursday, I phoned the Planning Officer, and I asked where the planning permission was because they were supposed to call me to give me a decision. They received too many applications, and they were understaffed. They told me that the decision will not be granted to me on that week and that there would have to be another couple of weeks to wait. I told them that I was about to lose the property I wanted to buy and put my business in jeopardy, but the woman said that there is nothing she can do.

On Friday I was supposed to call the lawyers and the estate agents, but I could not tell them anything, I just let it go. The whole weekend I was worried and thought 'now I am in trouble'. The business coach called me to ask if I got an answer, and I told him no, they did not have the chance to look at the application. He said, "well, that is good because if this does not go ahead, it means that God has something better for you". I did not have any faith in that answer, but on Monday when I came into work expecting to call, I found a letter from the Council saying that they had granted me my application and it was dated Friday. So, I did get the answer on Friday.

Because of his prayer and his certainty, I could move my business forward.

Later, I did find out who was trying to prevent me from buying the property, and it was one of my staff. I trained this person, and then he went to work for another local lab. That particular guy played golf with someone in the planning department, and it looked like his friend put my application to the end of the pile every week and never really got looked at.

An Alpha course led to Jesus

I decided to find out more about God. I did an Alpha course at a local church – it is a course where you have dinner with other people, and you have a bit of bible study. You get to ask questions and fellowship with other people that are Christians. In the third week, after listening to all the testimonies, I have decided that God must be true because all these people would not lie. Their stories convinced me to follow Jesus. I said the Sinner's prayer and then continued to the end of the course.

Finding God was a gradual thing for me, but since then, I have seen the power of God working in my life.

After that, this business coach got me into a good Christian church where I got some great Bible-based teachings, and I started to see God answering prayers.

Hamster brought back to life

I was only a year into faith when I sow our hamster who died and came back to life after I prayed. It did not live for long, but it was long enough for God to show me that He can raise the dead.

I sow the hamster dead in the morning, and my wife texted me during the day to ask me to bring a cage for the burial. When I came home at 11 pm, the hamster was dead for the whole day. Everyone was in bed. I remember I picked up the hamster, I held it in my hand, and as I was walking through the kitchen, I thought I am going to pray. I started to pray for this hamster in tongues and sow the eyes were opening. I thought "I must've squashed it a bit" and as I continued praying all this liquid came down my arm, it was like it was weeing down my arm. As I looked again, it convulsed, its body started to move. It did it three times, and then I saw it was breathing. He was not alive for long, but it was long enough for God to show me that He can bring life into a dead body. I put him back into the cage breathing, but I did not expect he would make it through the night, and he did not. This experience showed me that everything is possible with God.

After that, I have seen many healings. My stepdad had prostate cancer, and the doctors told him that he would need more chemo if his markers go up. I asked him not to do this, and I prayed for him. I also gave him some healing teaching to help him receive the healing. His markers went down, and he is still alive today. God did a miracle for him.

I have seen miracles in my family and on the street as well.

In terms of sensing the Holy Spirit, I always struggled with this, I never heard His voice in a way other people seem to hear, but I have seen the power of God working through my life.

I had a great journey meeting different people. He is alive, and He is on the Throne.

"You will receive power when the Holy Spirit comes on you, and you will be my witnesses in Jerusalem, and in all Judea and Samaria, and to the ends of the earth."

Acts 1:8

KNOW JESUS

We live in a broken world, and it does not take long to see this. Sexual assaults, abusive relationships, drugs, stealing, and robbery are just a few of the problems we see around us.

God did not plan this. When He made the world, He created it beautiful, full of love, with the purpose of people being close to Him. Adam and Eve had a perfect relationship with God. We were not designed to experience pain, suffering, and the brokenness that we see today, but people turned away from following God.

We are all humans, and when we experience all sorts of problems, we try to find a way out. We think partying, drugs and alcohol will fix the problem, but they do not do anything. Sometimes we get into wrong relationships hoping that this will be the way out, but the problem is still there. Whatever you try to do to come out of the situation you are in, you find yourself back on the wheel confronting the same problems.

God loved the world so much and suffered for seeing us pulling away from Him, and because He wanted us to come back to Him 2,000 years ago, Jesus paid the price for all the bad things people did, do, and will do in this life. *"He himself bore our sins' in his body on the cross, so that we might die to sins and live for righteousness; "by his wounds, you have been healed." –* 1 Peter 2:24.

Jesus preached a simple message. He asked us to believe and follow Him - *"For God so loved the world that he gave his one and only Son, that whoever believes in him shall not perish but have eternal life" – John 3:16*

"Repent, then, and turn to God, so that your sins may be wiped out, that times of refreshing may come from the Lord" – Acts 3:19.

If we choose to believe that Jesus died for your sins and receive forgiveness, God promised to forgive you and invite you to have a close relationship with Him. Your spirit will get born again and live in eternal in communion with God here and forever in heaven.

Through the power of the Holy Spirit, God will also change you to become a better person; He will be your guide, comforter, and teacher.

"If you declare with your mouth, "Jesus is Lord," and believe in your heart that God raised him from the dead, you will be saved. For it is with your heart that you

believe and are justified, and it is with your mouth that you profess your faith and are saved" – Romans 3:9-10

When we repent and believe in what Jesus did for us, God promised to heal us from the brokenness we live in and restore us to his design.

God has a good plan for your life, and after you turn to Him, He will have free reins to guide you. Believe in Him and get baptised.

As a child of God, you will have His favour and protection. He wants to guide you and help you fulfil your destiny. He will also give you the authority and the power to destroy the works of the devil in your life and other people's lives.

The reality is that we are either in one of these two places – in close relationship with God or against God. In which of these two places are you in today?

Is there anything holding you back from believing that Jesus died for your sins and that He wants to help you?

You can do this right now!

Take a moment and reflect on the way you lived your life and what are the things you wish you never did. God promised He would forgive and wipe away your sins. You will become a new creation and at Judgement, Day God will not judge you based on your sins but based on the righteousness in you – Jesus Christ.

Jesus has given us an invitation – *He said "Come to me, all you who are weary and burdened, and I will give you rest" – Matthew 11:28*

If you are ready to give your life to Jesus, pray this prayer with me:

Father God,

I believe that out of Your infinite love You have created me. I repent of every one of my sins. Please forgive me. Thank You for sending Jesus to die for me, to save me from eternal death. I want to turn to You and to place Jesus at the centre of my heart. I surrender to Him as Lord over my whole life.

I ask You to send me the gift of the Holy Spirit so that my life may be transformed.

In Jesus' name, I pray.

Amen!

If you have prayed this prayer and want to follow Jesus, I would love to hear from you. Please email me to carmen@jesusreignsmission.co.uk

Now that your spirit got born again and became a new creation, I recommend getting baptised with water (full immersion) and ask a Spirit-filled believer to pray for you to receive the baptism of the Holy Spirit.

When you go in the water, you die with Christ, and when you come out of the water, you raise with Christ. Now you are ready to live a new life in Christ. The old life has gone, the new life has just begun!

"We were therefore buried with him through baptism into death in order that, just as Christ was raised from the dead through the glory of the Father, we too may live a new life" – Romans 6:4.

Embrace a new journey as you discover how God sees you and who you are in Christ. You are His child, and you are victorious in all things through Jesus Christ who gives you strength.

ABOUT THE AUTHOR - Chosen and Called

My testimony is a story of finding a purpose after I received the love and the power of God. Looking back to how my life has been, I see that whenever something good happened in my life, God worked behind the scenes to guide and protect me. He did this all the time, but I was too blind to see His work. I took things for granted, and I did not know how to be grateful.

As a teenager and then a young adult, I was stubborn and only did what I wanted. Even though I achieved pretty much everything I set my mind to do, I cannot say I was content. Something was missing. I was too proud, arrogant at times, and I did not care much about other people. I did not feel any love or compassion for anyone. My family and I were all that mattered to me. I had friends but not one to go to if I had any problem.

I was always focused on my career and became a workaholic. At some point, I had three jobs – this was stressful and exhausting.

No personal relationship with God

I was born in Romania, got baptised as an infant, and grew up as an Orthodox. I used to say that I am a Christian, but I did not know God at all. I grew up in a typical family, where, like everyone, there were ups and downs. My parents supported me, gave me a good education and encouraged me to pursue my dreams at that time. Good or bad, they were my decisions, and no one could say anything. I did pretty much whatever I wanted to do. Thankfully, God protected me, and I did not do terrible things and what I did He forgave me. He always sent good people in my path to bring me back on the right track whenever I took a wrong turn.

I never questioned God's existence, but never had a personal relationship with Him. We were following the Orthodox traditions and never been encouraged to read the Bible. I do not think we had one at home. My mum taught me 'The Lord's prayer' when I was little, and I was reciting it like a poem every night before bedtime and first thing in the morning, without really paying any attention to the words I was saying. I was talking to an invisible God who was very distant to me. I believed He was somewhere up in Heaven above the sky. I used to pray to God in front of an anointed painting of Jesus, but I never felt His presence. As I grew up, I completely forgot about God. I stopped praying and going to church at all. I finished university and started writing for a local newspaper, then moved to another city, got married, and together we lived our lives as we wanted.

In May 2011, my husband and I moved to the UK, in Southampton, and, after moving here, somehow things started to fit into places. We received our visa sooner than expected, and my husband found a job quickly. I struggled a bit to settle, but things got better after a few months when I started working.

Two years later we decided it was time to have our own family, and in March 2013 our daughter was born.

God had a plan

One day in the summer of 2013, I took my daughter to the park and there I met Chantal, a wonderful lady, mum of three at that time. She was different than other people I knew - she was very joyful, did not gossip or complained about anything.

We became friends, and she never hid from me her love for Jesus. She encouraged me and prayed for me many times, and in December, she invited me to a Christmas service at her church. A few months after that, we moved to Swindon, where we stayed for a couple of years, but eventually, three years later, we returned to Southampton because God had a plan. He wanted me back there.

After returning to Southampton, my friend invited me to her church. I enjoyed the atmosphere, the music, and the people, but never heard any preaching because I was staying with my baby in the creche group. I was only going to church for my daughter and for the social aspect of being part of a community.

During this time, I started to question myself if there must be more to life than just going to work to earn a salary to pay the bills. My life had no purpose other than looking after my little family. I remembered that when I was young, I used to have high self-esteem believing I can achieve everything, but, after some disappointing work experiences in Romania and also in the UK, I stopped believing in myself. Being in a foreign country speaking with a Romanian accent did not help either. I wanted my confidence back.

The internet was full of information, so, in my search to understand how the Universe functions, how I can change myself and how I can change the things happening around me, I came across various techniques and practices related to personal development, Law of Attraction, and Mindpower. I tried them all, hoping to improve my life, find peace and a purpose. I watched the film 'The Secret' and started applying the Law of Attraction. It worked for a little while, but something was still missing. I moved into studying about Mindpower and became capable of controlling and blocking any toxic thoughts coming through my mind. Mastering this skill helped in one way, but it also made me more stressed. I was able to control the thoughts coming through my head but not my emotions. My heart was the same. Years later, I realised that out of the heart, the mouth speaks. Out of a bitter heart will only come angry words. Similarly, out of a joyful heart happy, encouraging words will come out.

I understood the laws of the universe after I turned to God. Jesus gave me the power and the keys to unlock my destiny, He gave me peace, love, but He also taught me how to be healed and live in divine healing and how to receive His blessings. All this is the result of having a close relationship with my Creator.

Today I only want to do what God wants me to do, and I live my life led by the Holy Spirit.

Intuition did not fail

From November 2016 to February 2017, I did not go to the church at all. Then, one morning I woke with the feeling that I had to go to the church the next Sunday because something good is going to happen and I would regret it if I do not go. I arranged for my husband to stay with our daughter, and I went to church – I was part of King's Community Church in Southampton. In his message, Pastor Ben Rowe shared the gospel, and he said that Jesus loves me and that He wants to be my best friend. When I heard this, I felt something I never experienced before. I felt warm on the inside, and I felt peace. I believed that Jesus wanted to be my best friend, and the very next day, I started talking to Him as if He was next to me.

I still did not understand why Jesus was so important and why everyone in church was lifting their hands praising Him, but I believed He is alive and He wants to be my friend. I suppose this was all I needed at that time. I started reading the New Testament, trying to find out more about Jesus – this time, the Bible made sense, and I loved it.

After I read how Jesus raised Lazarus from the dead, I had a clear vision – a fast-forward moving played in front of my eyes, and I saw myself raising a person who died in a car accident. It happened fast, and it looked so real. I believed that God will use me to do this one day. It did not occur until the moment I wrote this book yet, but I believe nothing is impossible for God. He used me to heal the sick and cast out demons, and I believe raising the dead is equally possible.

When I went to church next Sunday, the song 'No longer slaves' was played during the worship and tears started to roll down my cheeks (never happened this to me before in church). During this song, I told Jesus that I believe He died for me, I asked Him to forgive me, and I told Him I am going to follow Him and do whatever He wants me to do. I surrendered all to Him, and I asked Him to change me and make me a better person.

God became real to me

I continued seeking God, and I wanted the Holy Spirit that Jesus promised to give. My friend Chantal gave me a notebook and recommended me to write any revelations and thoughts I have regarding what I read in the Bible and what the Holy Spirit was telling me. On 8th March, I wrote a letter to God, asking Him to receive the baptism of the Holy Spirit. I did not know how this would happen.

The next day she invited me to her home and, out of nowhere, she told me she knew what I wanted. She did not know anything about the letter, but she knew I needed the Holy Spirit. When she prayed for me, I experienced the tangible presence of God. I felt like something was pulled out of my stomach, and heaviness was lifted. I was shaking and shivering, and I felt my hands being raised to worship Jesus, something I never did before. I left my friend's house feeling dizzy. I did not understand at that time what happened, but later I realised that Jesus set me free, and He filled me with the Holy Spirit.

The following morning I started to feel differently. I felt love and compassion for people, feelings I did not have before. I may have helped others, but only because it was something useful to do without coming from my heart. Being an only child, I cannot say I was too open to the idea of giving, sharing, helping. It was all about me, and everything was mine.

A few weeks later I got baptised in water. I believed I became a new creation because the Bible says so. I left my past behind, and I stopped feeling guilty for the things I have done and the wrong decisions I took in life. The baptism was beautiful, but sad at the same time because I did not have any family member with me.

When I got out of the water, I felt like my Heavenly Father was saying to me 'This is my beloved daughter of whom I am very pleased' like He told to people when Jesus came out of the water. My friend was with me, and she is supporting me up to this day.

Encounters with the living God

Giving my life to Jesus was the beginning of living a naturally supernatural life with Him every day. I say it is the best decision I took but, looking back, I can clearly see this was His plan. Jesus came after me. A few weeks after I got baptised, I remember walking back home from a prayer meeting when I heard a voice saying, "I have chosen you". It was so real that I turned around to look who said that. It was God speaking to me. A month later, I went to a conference organised by Global Awakening Europe. The presence of the Lord was so strong that my legs felt weak all the time. The Holy Spirit continued His work to deliver me and change me. There I received good teaching on healing and words of knowledge that helped me understand what was going on with me and that God wanted to heal the sick through me.

Other time, during a prayer meeting with some people from the church, I felt pain in the lower back and knowing that this could be a word of knowledge, I decided to check if anyone had that problem. I found out that someone sitting next to me had pain in the place I pointed to, and she got healed after I prayed for her. That was the moment when I realised how powerful Jesus and the name of Jesus are. I learnt from the Bible that I am supposed to pray with authority commanding the pain to go in the name of Jesus.

From this moment forward things started to move fast. The Holy Spirit became my companion. I was getting one step closer to God, and He was drawing five to me. I had a deep desire to be in His presence all the time and wanted to know Him better. I read the Bible daily, watched Andrew Wommack's preachings, and, day by day, my faith grew stronger and stronger.

One time my daughter had chapped lips and a patch of dark skin visible under her lips. As I prayed, I saw the skin coming back to standard colour and the lips getting moist. It happened quickly in front of my eyes. I have seen the healing power of God and understood how powerful the name of Jesus is.

Outside the house, God started showing me people to talk to and pray for them. I always found it hard to talk to strangers, especially on the streets, so this was challenging to me, but God continued His work, and this fear started to fade slowly. It disappeared completely when the Holy Spirit told me that is not about me and also that by doing what He tells me to do, I may save someone's life.

During this time, we found ourselves in financial difficulty. I could not find a job, and my husband was commuting many miles each day, which meant spending lots of money on petrol. I remember I applied for a job at the University of Southampton, and I was sure this job would be mine. I had the experience and the skills for it. However, one morning I felt that this job opportunity is not going to be mine. I was at home on my own, and, looking toward the ceiling, I asked God why do I feel that this job is not mine. I prayed for it and hoped to get it but, for some reasons, my gut feeling was saying that this job is not for me. I cannot say I expected an answer from God, but the answer came. It was as clear as someone talking to me - I heard "I have better plans for you". Soon after that, my husband received a pay rise, and we decided to move closer to his work. God showed me the house where He wanted us to move, and He made it possible for us to sign the contract without having any deposit at that moment.

After moving to Surrey, my daughter was on a waiting list for a place at the local school. I prayed for her to receive a place at this school before the start of the summer holiday. On Monday of the last week of school, they offered her the place, and she started school in September. The Holy Spirit led me to do things I did not know why I was doing them.

My UK experience was in organising events, but without realising it, after I gave my life to Jesus, I found myself connecting with different people online and became interested in learning how to use social media for business and web development. I have learnt new skills and even wrote a few books to help companies to promote their products or services online.

Two years later, I was offered a job in Digital Marketing without me looking for one, so I believe God wanted me to learn this because He knew what was going to come. In this workplace, God used me to bring hope, encouraging and praying for people.

In November 2017, I attended Power and Love school with Todd White and Robby Dawkins, and this was a life-changing moment for me. I enjoyed going out to pray for people – once you see the power of God flowing through you, you want more.

A new creation

Jesus not only paid the price for the wrongs things I did in my life, but He forgave me and accepted me into His family. He washed away all my sins, and I became a new creation. I believed this and never looked back.

I am a child of God, I am loved, blessed, accepted, forgiven, highly favoured, more than a conqueror, strong and courageous, and I can do all things through Christ who gives me strength.

I am a different person than I used to be. I behave differently than I used to before I gave my life to Jesus, and many other people who know me can testify this. The Holy Spirit works inside on me, changing me to become more like His Son.

The Word of God is my medicine and my sword against the devil. We live in this world, but there is also a spiritual world surrounding us.

Jesus gave us authority against the darkness, and I do not hesitate to use it for other people and me.

156

Healed!

I saw great results in my life from trusting God and believing that every single word in the Bible is true and that it applies to me. If you are a Christian or you just decided now to follow Jesus, the promises of God belong to you as well, including Isaiah 55:4 which says that Jesus bore our sicknesses and He carried our pains. When you receive Jesus as your Lord and Saviour, you can also receive the healing and the freedom He paid the price for.

I used to suffer from hyperthyroid for many years, and no medication seemed to work. In Romania, I ended up in the hospital with a severe allergy from the pills I was taking. Years later, when my daughter was a baby, the doctors asked me to either have surgery to have my thyroid removed or go through radioactive iodine to destroy it. The surgeon asked me to do this because there was a high risk for my liver to get damaged if I would continue taking the same high-dose of medications for a long time.

I declined both procedures, believing that Jesus died for this and that I could receive my healing through faith like the woman with the issue of blood mentioned in the Bible (Matthew 9:20–22). At that time, I was also listening to Andrew Wommack's teachings called 'You already got it' and 'God wants you well', which I am sure helped me see that God wanted me healed.

I took a radical decision and stopped the medication entirely without telling anyone. When the symptoms appeared, I commanded them to go in the name of Jesus, as Peter did when he healed a beggar. I thanked God every day, multiple times a day, that He already healed me, and declared Isaiah 55:3 - 4 over me. Forty days later, more or less, I was due for a review, and the blood tests came normal. For me, this was the confirmation that I got healed. It took almost 40 days for my body to align with the Will of God and see the healing manifested. Two months after I was officially discharged from the hospital records and never had any problems with my thyroid since.

I believe God wants me well, and I do not accept any pain or medical problem. Whenever the enemy tries to attack my health, I command the symptoms to go, in the name of Jesus.

In 2019 I ended up in the hospital with severe stomach pain, and, after further investigations, the doctors found out that I had pancreatitis caused by gallstones. I prayed that night, and the blood tests came with normal values the next day. The pancreatitis was gone. They did a scan and discovered lots of gallstones of various sized, and there was no treatment other than gallbladder removal.

I did not feel good about having my gallbladder removed, so I declined the surgery and chose to believe the Bible – if God says He healed me 2,000 years ago because of what Jesus did, I decided to accept this and do what I did with the hyperthyroid. I did not have any more pain for over a year (until I started writing this book). I did not do any scan, but I know I am healed.

I do not recommend stopping any medication or declining any surgery, but I encourage you to spend time with God and read what the Bible says on healing until you see for yourself what the Will of God is. I spent thousands of hours doing this. *"Faith comes by hearing, and hearing by the word of God"* (Romans 10:17, NKJV).

You shall receive POWER

Christianity without having a personal relationship with Jesus and without being filled with the Holy Spirit, is just a religion. To live a peaceful, joyful and powerful life you need Jesus. He helped many other people I know and me.

If you read the Bible, you are probably familiar with Acts 1:8 – *"you will receive power when the Holy Spirit comes on you"*. It is a promise, and the Lord will be pleased to send you the Holy Spirit if you ask Him.

The decision is yours if you want to believe that Jesus loves you and that He died for you.

Today I am no longer worried, stressed, or anxious about anything because I know I can trust God. Love, joy, peace, patience, and kindness are part of my being. I do not have to try to feel these feelings as I used to do when practising Mindpower and Law of Attraction. The Holy Spirit did it all for me, as He deposited this in my Spirit. My job now is to stay close to God, the source of the power that dwells inside of me.

I am a child of God, and I know what belongs to me, and what my God-given purpose is. I learnt from the Bible how to walk in divine healing and how to pray to have my prayers answered. Most importantly, I trust God, and I believe He will turn things around for His glory and also to guide and protect me. He is directing my steps. *"I have been crucified with Christ, and I no longer live, but Christ lives in me. The life I now live in the body, I live by faith in the Son of God, who loved me and gave himself for me"* – *Galatians 2:20.*

There is no greater joy than knowing that Jesus is inside of me, and the Holy Spirit can guide me at every step.

I have seen the power of God working in my life and other people's lives as I prayed for them.

I love God the Father, Jesus, and the Holy Spirit, and also the Bible, which is my manual to live my life by. Christians are supposed to live by faith and not by sight, trusting God at every step but also knowing His promises and being filled with the Holy Spirit.

I believe God's ways are better than mine, and my husband and I chose to leave our lives led by the Holy Spirit. God's ways are already blessed. It is better to do what He has planned for you instead of choosing what you want and trying to get His blessing.

Today I have a close relationship with God and the Holy Spirit is my guide, my teacher, and my comforter. I do not do anything until I check if that is what God wants me to do, and I assure you that whenever I did what God told me the outcome was great. I walked in favour, and He opened doors for me. He cares about my family and provides for us and for the work I do for Him.

In June 2020, during the lockdown, the Lord told me to gather His co-workers and send them into His harvest fields. This is how the ministry Jesus Reigns Mission came into existence. We are disciples and ambassadors for Christ that encourage each other to live an evangelistic lifestyle every day and represent Jesus wherever we go.

"Very truly I tell you, whoever believes in me will do the works I have been doing, and they will do even greater things than these because I am going to the Father. And I will do whatever you ask in my name, so that the Father may be glorified in the Son. You may ask me for anything in my name, and I will do it" - John 14:12-14.

God will remove your past and help you start anew. Satan wants to kill and destroy people, but Jesus came to give us life to the full. Choose to believe this and give Jesus a chance. Repent, get baptised and follow Him.

If you are still not sure if Jesus can help you, you can ask Him to reveal Himself to you. Many of the people that shared their stories in this book did it.

A close friend to me had some specific prayers that looked almost impossible to be answered. She put God to the test, but He was so merciful that He responded to all her prayers.

See below her testimony:

"I started to question if Jesus is alive, if He died for my sins, if He loves me and if He is the Lord and Saviour I need. Trying to find out an answer I came up with a plan. I told Jesus that I have three things I would like to ask Him to do, and if He answers my prayers, I will believe He is real, and I will follow Him. My prayers were specific – I asked Jesus to make a way to receive a work contract I have been waiting for a long time, for my husband to be promoted at work and for a friend to recover well after a severe accident – he was in a coma with a life support machine when I prayed. To make it more challenging, I told Jesus I would give Him a week to answer my prayers. Somehow, I believed He would do it. By Friday next week, exactly one week after I prayed, God has been answering all my prayers. Not one of them was missing. I received my contract; my husband got promoted at work and took a new position in the company and the friend I prayed for came to life. At that moment, I believed that Jesus was real. I started to cry of happiness because I could not believe it. He answered all my prayers, and I gave my life to Jesus. A couple of months later, I got baptised, and today I believe and trust Him".

If this book helped you in any way, please leave a review on the platform you bought it from and tell other people about it.

Hope is the blueprint of faith.

"Faith is confidence in what we hope for and assurance about what we do not see" – *Hebrews 11:1.*

Carmen Lascu leads a team of born again Christians who go out on the streets of Staines to share the gospel, heal the sick and pray for people. She is also connected with other disciples of Christ from London and other towns that walk in love and power, in the name of Jesus and empowered by the Holy Spirit.

She loves God and is passionate about encouraging born again Christians to step out of their comfort zone and live a supernatural lifestyle every day doing what Jesus and the first disciples did – proclaiming and demonstrating the Kingdom of God on the streets and wherever they go. We are called to bring a message of hope, love and peace into the world as we carry the presence of God wherever we go.

Please visit www.jesusreignsmission.co.uk if you want to stay connected with this ministry and Carmen's personal website where she shares about her faith, business and home education – www.carmenlascu.co.uk

Printed in Great Britain
by Amazon

78866062R00098